Personal Momentum

Secrets of Self-Transformation

Your 30 day
CHANGE FOR LIFE
Program

Natan Verkhovsky, M.Ht

Copyright © Natan Verkhovsky 2020

All rights reserved. No part of this publication may be reproduced or transmitted in any form or by any means, electronic or mechanical, including photocopy, recording, or any information storage or retrieval system, without written permission from the publisher.

The author does not intend to provide any advice, psychological or otherwise , and does not prescribe the use of any methods in this book as form of treatment for mental, or physical ailments. The author assumes no responsibility for the readers decisions, actions or choices.

First edition.

ISBN 978-0-6487192-6-7

Cover by Lorenza Minghetti

To My Mother: Who's always wanted her son to be a writer and has been an inspiration, and a pillar of strength and goodness all my life! What a kind and loving light! Thank you for enveloping me in your love!

To My Father: Who's shown me what it takes to be a real gentleman, and that life balance is truly living in love and spreading light in all your relationships, and that is the happiest and healthiest way to be the 'being' in human being.

To My Brother: One of my lifelong, closest possible friends and someone who gets me at a completely different level than any other human being on Earth - I love you so much! Thanks for always making me want to do more, be more and love more!

To My Wife: Who has been my guiding light, my moral compass and my heart when I can't find mine. Thank you for loving me so brilliantly! I can't help feel shiny and new every time you look at me!

To My Daughter: Whom I'd love to show that anything is possible...if you live in love and follow and share your light! You are an incredible and truly beautiful person, inside and out - you are full of such awesomeness!

CONTENTS

INTRODUCTION	1
PROLOGUE	9
HOW TO USE THIS BOOK	13
THE STRESS RESISTANT PERSONALITY	18
PERSONAL MOMENTUM - AT A GLANCE	19
INTENTION	23
Personal mastery exercises for intention	31
Specialized routine to increase intention	32
INTENSITY	35
Personal mastery exercises for intensity	42
Specialized routine to increase intensity	44
PRODUCTIVITY	49
Personal mastery exercises for productivity	59
Specialized routine to increase productivity	61
CHECKLIST FOR SUCCESS	65
NIGHT-TIME MANTRA SYSTEM	67
EPILOGUE	73
RESOURCES	77
Stress Quiz	79
Workplace Quiz	83
Daily Tracksheets & Success Journal	89
(Days 1 to 30)	
ABOUT THE AUTHOR	211

TESTIMONIALS

"This book is awesome; it dives into the mysterious world of the fundamental building blocks of life. Natan gives you the blueprint and tools to reprogram yourself and your life, creating amazing results in attaining your personal greatness. Much like pulling back the curtain to reveal the magic, this work is a fundamental step to understanding oneself and life! A definite must read!"
- *Carolyn Raymond, Medical Supplies Contract Specialist*

"Personal Momentum" does exactly what the subtext implies; these secrets will transform your life! I know this because the principles contained therein changed me forever! You will learn tools, techniques, and strategies that when applied, will change everything from negative thoughts to eliminating the habits that do not serve you. Do you want to become the best possible version of yourself? This book will facilitate those changes within you! Natan, is a master presenter, teacher, and practitioner! His writing style is easy to read, understand and implement. In my opinion, you will find it difficult to find someone as qualified to facilitate your transformation than Natan Verkhovsky!
- *David Adams, Founder and CEO, People Steward Leadership*

"Natan has created an inspiring guide full of practical exercises to help all of us to realign our energy, intentions, and the actions we take in our lives to achieve our goals."
- *Wanda V. Chaves, Ph.D. Clinical Associate Professor of Management, University of South Carolina*

"Congratulations Natan on presenting your vision, content and inspiration in a practical, step by step, interactive manner. Amazing insights, terrific experiences, and wonderful techniques that are relevant, uplifting and truly transformational. I highly recommend this book to anyone undergoing changes in their life and those who want to take charge of their life journey."
- *Dave Rogers, International Best Selling Author & Coach*

"Although I am a confident person and had experienced a significant number of personal development courses prior to working with Natan, I sensed there was something holding me back and knew there was definitely room for change in my life. I met Natan through a recommendation from a friend and was immediately drawn to his fun, engaging, and compassionate personality. At first, I was hesitant, as I knew very quickly that working with Natan would mean making a huge commitment to myself, and that his highly professional and personalized approach would mean big changes in my perception of what is possible for me. Having now worked with Natan, I'm excited about the passion, intensity, and productivity he has helped me bring to my life. I've really only just begun to bring peak-performance and excellence into every day but with the tools, drills and exercises I now incorporate, I feel so much more powerful and in control of my choices. So, if you're considering taking your life to the next level, I have no doubt that Natan can get you there. I highly recommend working with him in any way you can......and be prepared for change!"

- *Tracey Regan, Author/Director, The Lemon Tree Book Company Ltd.*

"In my experience, when material is derived from experimentation and practice, it is always reassuring. Even though the initial application of these techniques was high performance sports-related, the eventual transfer of that know-how to the business world and how it can impact an individual's everyday life, has proven to offer very effective and practical skills. There is much to learn from here, and to enjoy the results of practicing the exercises."

- *Boris Verkhovsky, Former National Coach, Master Course Conductor, Director Expert - Cirque du Soleil*

FOREWORD
- by Tracey Regan

No matter where you are in life, or what age, change is inevitable. In fact, most people go through noticeably big changes in their lives every 7-10 years. These changes can be a choice, or more often in my experience at least, they come out of nowhere and turn your whole world upside down. You're quietly moving through life, 'mostly' believing you've got what you want, then 'BAM', something happens to knock the wind from your sails and it's as if you have to pick yourself up and start again.

These moments of turmoil can have a massive impact. Many people experience depression, anxiety and even 'breakdown' during these times.

However, what if you had the tools and strategies to face these challenges head-on? What if you could experience growth from these events and learn valuable lessons to enhance your life? And what if you could anticipate change, or even design the life you want and make changes of your own choice?

Well, you're in luck! If you've picked up this amazing book, 'Personal Momentum', you're in for an incredible ride of self-discovery and you'll find that change is so much easier than you thought.

When I started to work through the program myself, I quickly realized that it would be life-changing. This program is so simple in it's approach to change, and yet so powerful. I've been on my own journey of self-discovery for the last decade, and experienced healing and growth in many forms, but this is the first time I have felt so much peace and contentment with myself, in control of my emotions and my life.

In this book you will find strategies, drills and techniques that Natan has used in over 20 years of coaching professional athletes, CEO's and peak performers. These strategies have been developed and grown over time, and have been selected to provide maximum effect.

I also encourage you to complete your daily tracksheets and success journal every day. At first, you may wonder about the value of recording so much information during your day, but I guarantee that around Day 10, you will start to see patterns that will bring amazing clarity and lead you to unexpected awareness, to launch your momentum for change.

As you work through the program, you'll find Natan's passion, and compassion, is infectious and as you start to use these techniques every day, I have no doubt your life will change for the better.

Prepare yourself for an adventure and enjoy the journey!

*When things change inside you,
things change around you
~ unknown*

INTRODUCTION

Have you ever considered that with billions of people on Earth, no two people in the history of time have ever had the same fingerprints, or the same DNA?

Each and every one of us are completely unique and individual!

So are you acting as your most unique self? If we are such islands of individuality, why do we wish to mirror our neighbor? More importantly, if our biological blueprints call for billions of one-of-a-kind individuals in this world, then why the overwhelming desire, even the imperative need to connect to others, to socialize, to be accepted by and belong with our peers?

All of us are just living our lives through our own perceptions and experiences. We are creating our life stories, which in turn create our personal beliefs. Ultimately, this is so we can justify and defend our decisions and prejudices.

Each of our experiences and perceptions, particularly during moments of great stress, can lock in an emotion with an anchor

As an example, consider a woman enduring a long, painful dental surgery. The pain and trauma of this event is emotionally remembered for a lifetime. Yet a whole new world of pain opens up to that same woman during childbirth, and she will often be able to smile, years later, as she recounts her labor ... but not her dental surgery.

Neither good nor bad feelings were attached to the child before the moment of birth. Her state of mind was focused and driven with single-minded ruthlessness to the task of giving birth. It must be in that instant, that our brain can not think in a cognitive manner, that our very essence becomes so absorbed in the task at hand that the conscious mind seems to be riding on autopilot, as every fiber of our being is united in the task, whatever that may be.

It would be reasonable to ask, "How could one experience, dental surgery considerably weaker in pain and intensity, be so much more traumatic than childbirth, especially when the latter experience is infinitely more painful and intense?"

The key lies in a point of relativity. It is exactly because giving birth is infinitely more important than dental surgery. Somehow, deep down the mother-to-be knows this. Giving birth means more to the woman than a root canal. No one can deny this. And it's exactly because of this, that she can empower herself from the experience, altering her perception from one of 'trauma' to one of 'strength'.

The experience can alter deep-down core perceptions that have previously been held as personal beliefs. The change empowers her and reinforces her enough to help maintain that change in her beliefs.

That is as simple and as hard as it is

The process of taking a traumatic, painful event and re-wiring it as something empowering, becomes a great rite of passage; one you feel honored, and proud to have taken.

We have to upset some deep fundamental beliefs in order to accomplish that which we currently feel is 'impossible'. Can we transform ourselves from uninitiated possessors of our bodies and minds to become truly enlightened beings? Beings who seamlessly unify mind, body, and spirit, touching our very hearts.

Could we do more and be more than we currently are?

If you could catapult to your most evolved, highest state of being, right now, would it be where you are now, being who you are now? Imagine if you could tap into a reservoir of inner energy to assist in transforming into something you could be truly proud of. A seamless being, where mental, physical, emotional, sexual, spiritual, social, financial and personal spheres of influence, all merge and each adds to the total power of you. Instead, we become filled with worry after worry and end up ignoring so many facets of ourselves. There are parts of us that we simply don't explore.

To do more with what we have requires a shift in faith

For a shift to take place, we need to address the pain that change inevitably brings, and be prepared to answer some hard personal questions. Working through this program you will inevitably ask yourself, "Why am I doing this?"

The answer will have to be a powerful and persuasive one, strong enough to get you through the confusion and frustration that comes with change.

Only your conviction will get you through the worst of it.

When we turn to that which makes us different from all others in the world, the experience of turning within, the very act itself – no matter how we experience it – enlightens us. It shows us how to better interact with the rest of the world.

When we find a quiet inner place, we soon discover the duality of being: 'no one is like me'/'I am like no one,' and 'everyone is like me'/'I am like everyone else'. Couldn't all conditions co-exist within you simultaneously? Maybe we can learn to use a little more insight in the pursuit of the infinite energy that exists within us all, instead of the pursuit of instant gratification.

Did you know, that most of us are using less than 10% of our mental & physical abilities?

In times of great duress, humans have shown the ability to be able to tap into incredible states of mental, physical and emotional power. We can learn to harness that power, that energy and be able to call upon it at will. Athletes call that state 'being in the zone'; everything slows down, you seem to see things before they happen, you are relaxed, calm, cool, and collected. And the amount of strength you can summon during these moments is legendary.

We can all swiftly call upon a more primal state of being in which we can do away with the insecurities and doubts that are ever-present in normal thinking, and summon cunning, courage, and awareness. Awareness. That's what it's all about.

What you focus on is what you get

Awareness is a bizarre concept. Maybe because we choose to ignore it for most of our lives. If someone were to ask where you come from, how you got here, and what your purpose is, most of us would be hard-pressed to answer. We would have to ponder on it. If we are asked 'who we are,' we are more likely to go to 'what we do!'

Yet to answer truthfully, 'who we are' is so very much closer to the heart of the matter. We never actually answer the question when someone asks who we are. We always give some cop-out answer like, "My name is...," but they didn't ask us about 'my' anything. That was not the real question. It was your purpose that was being examined to see if you could be trusted.

When someone asks any question, they are actually focused on everything you are not saying! They want to know how you hold yourself when you answer and how enthusiastic you are about what you do. They want insight into who you really are.

We are all physical, electrical, and chemical

We walk around in time and space just like an inanimate machine. That which is operating the material and physical body is called spirit, soul, consciousness, or whatever pleases you. You are clearly so much more than your physical body and your mental processes. You are part of creation and part of the universe. This is a fact. Just by being alive you already satisfy both requirements. But why are you so important?

Your individuality is so important that you have your own voice and fingerprints to ensure your uniqueness. This should tell you something.

Think about why you are not like anyone else on Earth and if you find out why, act like it. You are meant to be different. Enjoy the journey.

In order to fully be all that you can be, you have to use your mind and body as one.
It's easier than you think.
Your mind and body are totally linked

You know this must be true, if you don't, try to consciously stop breathing and see how long that lasts. Your body will override your wishes and force you to breathe. Why is there a cut-off point? Can you override this or any other automatic bodily function? Sometimes, if you have all the proper circumstances in place, you can reprogram any part of yourself. People have eradicated cancer from their bodies and yet there is a great deal of doubt left about our own abilities. In the process of searching out our meanings we are busy making other plans.

Each of us creates our own 'life stories'. These stories contain and explain our personal beliefs, justify and defend our positions, decisions and the lives we consciously choose to create. On the 'headshrinkers' couch, a client recounts their 'life story' in search of insights. This recounting process can further make the person feel like a helpless victim of the past. All the pain and the problems begin to make some twisted sort of sense. Assigning and accepting blame can often be the only outcome.

If you want to change your future,
change your thinking
– starting right now

You are what you think. You know this is true. And in order to override your body's automatic programming, the "autopilot" function of the subconscious, you must first create a great deal of ceremony and fascination for the subconscious to be fully involved.

It only takes an instant in real-life time to make a conscious decision, a choice

Internally, that may seem like an eternity if you don't use the "turbo" function of your subconscious that is inside each and every one of us from birth. The process of change is simple and requires minimal effort and time, you just have to give it the proper mental perception, much like you subconsciously did when you were an infant, learning about the world around you. If as an infant your parents could have communicated clear instructions directly to your subconscious mind, in a way you could have understood, maybe you could have learned to walk or talk much earlier.

Now you can be an enlightened parent to yourself, and like a child, mold yourself to whatever image you wish. You can learn new things the way an infant would, and be open and curious to the world around you. Luckily it's never too late. The only real question left is, "What are you waiting for?"

Natan Verkhovsky, M.Ht
Medical Hypnotherapist
Mental Training Specialist

Prologue :
Happiness = Progress

When it comes to Happiness, I look back on a very interesting man who was a peak performance client of mine. He was 110% convinced that 'he' was the most successful person he knew. He was also 110% convinced that he was miserable and just couldn't figure out why.

For him, his morning ritual was to check things off his list! He would check off how beautiful his wife was, how brilliant his kids were and how much they adored him. He would check off his millions of dollars in the bank, his cars, boats, planes, vacation properties, the works. When he first came to me, he said, "I've got six-pack abs, I've climbed Mount Everest, I can hold my breath for $4 \frac{1}{2}$ minutes, I've accomplished so much and achieved every success, but I'm just feeling more and more miserable. I can't understand it."

He was doing the exercise every morning of focusing on all he had done and all his acquisitions, and it was having a negative effect. He was trying to get more 'with-out' himself, rather than going 'within' himself. For him, he had never really taken a look at what was the source of his happiness and when he spoke with me he was surprised.

I asked him a few simple questions. "When was the last time you progressed? When was the last time you challenged yourself and rose to that challenge? A time you truly put yourself in a vulnerable position, and you weren't 100% sure of yourself? When did you have to pull something from deep within, while all the time doubting yourself? When did you have a goal that you didn't think you could achieve, but you went the extra mile, dug deep and did it even though you didn't think you could? When was the last time you truly pushed yourself, moved forward and accomplished anything?"

He was stunned and a little upset at first, but then he realized what I was saying. "Wow," he said, "you're right. It's been ages since I truly challenged myself. I thought I was doing things differently, but really, every new pursuit, every acquisition was the same as I've been doing for years. It was always something I knew I could do. I was never putting myself out of my comfort zone."

He sat quietly for a moment, and then added, "The times I remember that I've been really happy, there's been a struggle, a pursuit, a chase, a bit of a hunt. I've always enjoyed things that weren't so easy for me, but I never really thought about it like that." I told him that happiness is something that is different for everyone. In a room of a hundred people, each one of us could have a different thing that makes us happy.

However, I also believe that there is one thing that would apply to every one of us, and that is 'Happiness equals Progress'. Every time you progress, move forward, or challenge yourself and rise to the occasion, there is a beautiful moment of pure happiness.

Whenever you look at your life and you can't seem to find happiness, go challenge yourself. Put yourself into the fight, give yourself something to conquer, put yourself outside of your comfort zone and step up to the challenge. When you achieve that which you thought you couldn't, you will smile really deeply, straight from your heart, and you will feel true happiness.

The new thought of challenging himself, made him feel happy even in that moment. He immediately set forward on what he knew was the most challenging thing for him at the time, which was public speaking. It was terrifying for him, but he relished in that terror, because he understood that his happiest moments were when he stepped out of his comfort zone.

He quickly learned how to become 'comfortable being uncomfortable' and it was the most powerful realization that would change the rest of his life.

HAPPINESS EQUALS PROGRESS is a wonderful checkmark to see if you are truly moving forward. And if you are, you should be very happy.

"Happiness is when what you think, what you say, and what you do, are in harmony."

~ Ghandi

Program Instructions
How To Use This Book!

Your Personal Momentum program will take several weeks to become fully effective. You may see results almost immediately, but most of us need more time to let everything sink in, just like antibiotics that need a few days to establish themselves in your system, before becoming dominant, and then build up in concentration and intensity as the weeks go on.

That's why your doctor always tells you to finish the prescription even if you feel better. The medication has to run it's course or it's dangerous to your body. This program is like the above example in that the more effort you spend, and the more time you give to the theory and exercises, the more results you'll see. There are more things going on than appear evident in terms of changing the 'old' you into the 'new' you.

A duck on a pond appears graceful and stoic as it glides effortlessly across the water, underneath the surface – it's paddling like hell

That's what your change is like. But once your mind truly and fully accepts the new you and sees you as clearly as a photograph, then your body can go about following that picture. Emotional fuel is added as you visually confirm that changes are actually taking place, which in turn will speed up the whole process.

It all begins with getting your mind to accept the possibility of change in the first place

That's when everything looks like the duck on the surface of the pond; calm and yet purposeful, with direction. What it took to get you there is what the duck looks like under the surface of the water. Everyone is a little different in regard to what it takes to trigger their brain into believing they are truly capable of change.

Your change may be triggered by doing something new or by ingraining a new pattern of behaviour through repetition of something you've been doing already. Everyone is different and needs a differing amount of time and dedication to a task to see its results.

Only doing something different today than you did yesterday can bring you something new

If you repeat the same thing today, tomorrow you get the same results. If you do something different today, tomorrow you will have different results.

If you're like most people, by now you're pretty excited about the possibilities of a whole new you

Over the next several weeks, you will have to come to terms with yourself and what you really want to happen here. This is your own personal Mt. Everest. Your own Boot Camp, Warrior Elite Training. Your own personal Alice-in-Wonderland Looking Glass. Your Sanctuary, Refuge, Mecca, Temple, Shrine. Here we let you get to the heart of who you really are. Here we test you, break you down, and build you up stronger, faster, and smarter than ever. Better than you ever thought you could be.

We suggest you enjoy the process of changing any which way you feel most comfortable. Some of you will jump right into self re-programming, while others like to start a little slower. Some pick smaller, more noticeable goals to "see" if the program works.

*Without getting ahead of ourselves, let's concentrate on your problem in bite- sized pieces.
Let's break it down to its chief components :*

Intention, Intensity and Productivity

This is all related to your personal activation level of stress. Some people work best around 7-8 out of 10 on the stress scale and others work best around 3-4 out of 10. Energy is the secret ingredient in perfect time management. When it seems as if there aren't enough hours in a day, what you really need is more energy, not more time.

With optimal levels of energy you can even get more done in less time. The trick seems to be in controlling what level of stress activates your personal state of peak performance. This is different for each of us. Certain levels of stress seem to trigger anxiety and tension, make you feel run-down all the time and drain your immune system's reserves.

Any stress can have powerful repercussions, mentally, emotionally, and physically. This is why a complete set of Mental, Physical and Emotional exercises, drills and techniques have been designed specifically to increase energy, reduce stress and eliminate tension and anxiety.

Through learning these exercises, their guidelines and practical applications, you will learn to find and control what level of stress activates your optimal state of performance. The increase in energy will help keep you in a state professional athletes call, 'The Zone'. Everything slows down yet you seem to speed up, and every task is made that much easier. This can have a compounding affect and help erase the negative effects of previous stressors.

One way to counter stress is to re-energize with the obvious combination of good eating, good sleeping, multi-vitamins, and physical exercise. But what if you are already eating, sleeping and exercising well? Perhaps there is an alternative system of generating and maintaining energy levels. That's where this program can help!

The 'Secrets to Self-Transformation' program is highly successful if used properly

Part of your change will have to be mental, part of it physical, and an emotional component is always present. By combining techniques on all three fronts, a focused effort takes place. We include N.M.S. (a Night-time Mantra System) and Power Goal Cards, so that when you've gone through the process of change, you can duplicate your efforts with other changes you've always wanted to make - now faster and easier due to the programming already being in place.

Did you know?.... The last thing the mind focuses on as it falls asleep, loops through your mind over and over - all night long

This is the secret to subconscious programming; it's how it's possible to learn a new language in a month, and that's how your N.M.S. Power Goal Cards work too.

Along with the N.M.S. and Power Goal Cards, there is a 'resources' section, where you can record your level of intention, intensity and productivity at different times throughout the day. You should also record your daily highs, lows and personal revelations. For your awareness, it really is important to write down and track your emotions daily. While improving your mental skills, you take a hands-on approach to your emotional and physical cravings that may come and tempt you. Each section also has techniques and exercises that you can use to fix and heal your past, curb your current destructive desires, and prepare you for the glorious new you that awaits.

As it takes the mind and body approximately 21-30 days and nights to fully absorb change and create a new habit, you must prepare yourself for a one-of-a-kind adventure of self-discovery

From all those who have come before you, comes a word of advice to get you through the worst of the turbulence that change will inevitably bring over the next few weeks.

BELIEVE!
FULLY AND COMPLETELY.
BELIEVE IN YOURSELF LIKE NEVER BEFORE.
YOU'VE COME SO FAR, YOU CAN DO THIS.
YOUR BODY IS RUN BY YOUR MIND AND
YOUR MIND IS RUN BY YOUR BELIEFS.
BELIEVE!

The Stress-Resistant Personality

The fundamental requirement for having a happy and productive life, and to lower toxic stress levels that have physical repercussions on our bodies, is to develop a 'stress resistant personality'.

Fortunately, you can beat stress, anxiety and build resilience to weather life's storms, with proven positive mental exercises and techniques that can be learned.

Set peace of mind as your highest goal, and organize your life around it!
~ Brian Tracy

Psychologists agree* that people with resilience and high levels of stress but low levels of illness, share three characteristics:

CONTROL
a sense of purpose and direction in life

COMMITMENT
to work, hobbies, social life or family

CHALLENGE
seeing changes in life as normal and positive, rather than a threat

*ref : https://thriveglobal.com/stories/how-to-incorporate-the-three-c-s-of-resilience-into-your-life/
https://www.mentaltoughness.partners/the-4-c/
https://psycentral.wordpress.com/2012/09/14/coping-change-psychological-hardiness-dr-gary-wood-psychology-coaching/

Personal Momentum
- at a glance!

An increase in INTENTION

Principles of Intention & Desire
- Effectiveness is the measure of truth
- The world is what you think it is
- Your Intention dictates your reality

Specialized routine to increase INTENTION
- Energy Assessment Drill
- Biofeedback Breathing Exercise
- Blackboard Hi-Lite Exercise
- Success Vault Drill
- Intense Memory Recall Drill
- Pre-Performance visualization
- Post-Performance visualization

Personal mastery exercises for intention.

PLUS - an increase in INTENSITY

Principles of Intensity = Power
- All power comes from within
- NOW is the moment of power
- F.E.A.R. is nothing more than a False Education Appearing Real
- Basic rules of subconscious modification programming

Specialized routine to increase INTENSITY
- Energy Assessment Drill
- Centering Drill
- Concentrated Breathing Exercise
- Mental Scream Drill
- Targeting Exercise

Personal mastery exercises for intensity.

EQUALS - an increase in *PRODUCTIVITY*

Principles of Productivity & Energy
- The energy of your body is totally controlled by the intention of your mind
- The more Points of Reference you create, the farther out of your paradigm you can go and safely return.
- Your energy flows where your attention goes

Specialized routine to increase PRODUCTIVITY
- Energy Assessment Drill
- Facial self-massage
- Biofeedback Breathing Exercise
- Inner Body Visualization
- Random Escape Visualization

Personal mastery exercises for productivity.

INTENTION

The Principles of Intention & Desire

A Case Study

I had a client who was a strong, very 'manly' man. He had previously worked as a rigger for Cirque Du Soleil and in his job would move hundreds of pounds of rope with his bare hands. There was a little bit of 'machoism' when we first started working together, but he quickly put that barrier down when he realized I had no hidden agenda.

When he started to communicate a little more, I could tell when he was getting close to what he really needed to say, as he would start to get choked up, to the point where he couldn't speak. I asked him what had happened.

He told me that he'd had throat cancer, and an operation to remove it. Everything had healed, and he was in remission, but he was experiencing a lot of worry that it may come back.

As we talked a little more, and started to do some in-depth therapy, we were able to understand his intention. We discovered that he found strength in his life through negative reinforcement. He was constantly telling himself he was not enough, not good enough, not worthy.

He was smoking more than two packs a day, prior to his throat cancer, yet even his smoking hadn't made him feel lighter, or better. He smoked with 'bad intention', in a way that was toxic, and not just from the chemicals.

Deep down inside, he felt a genuine responsibility, and tried to take ownership of his negative self-talk. He was constantly, and chronically, feeling guilty for the way he was focusing all his attention on his feelings of 'not being enough.'

All those years of constant guilt will at some point manifest to the nearest physical equivalent in the body. Throat cancer was his manifestation of the guilt that he had focused on for so long when he spoke so negatively to himself. And he had been doing this for decades without any awareness of what he was doing.

It wasn't just the bad habit of smoking, but the bad intention behind the way he smoked, that needed to change. Without taking away the bad intention, he would just replace smoking with another activity. And even if that activity was a good habit, let's say exercise, if done with bad intention, he would just overdo it, over-use his muscles and constantly be judging himself unfairly. With that intention, even a good habit would hurt him, as he would be trying to live up to some ideal that is not possible or true.

Once we uncovered the root of the feelings, and took away all the negativity, he was able to remove the bad intention. His intention once clarified, ensured that the healing white light that was needed, penetrated every orifice and inside every organ until he was 100% guilt-free.

He finally gave himself permission to let go and forgive himself, which stopped him feeling like he wasn't enough, and he began to feel the abundance that he was enough, and deserved every happiness.

Effectiveness Is The Measure Of Truth

From birth until death, everything in your life moves in the direction of your most dominant thought! If as a child your attention focused on certain events for long enough - remember it only takes 21-30 days to form a habit - then it was implanted as a behaviour pattern and your reality was altered, ready to be re-set and replaced at any time by something more efficient.

Imagine that there is no longer a correct or incorrect to ANYTHING! No right or wrong way to do or say anything, where everything is measured in levels of effectiveness and efficiency.

Imagine if you replace the word 'WRONG' with 'Ineffective' or 'Inefficient'

If you replace the word 'wrong' in your subconscious and instead use 'ineffective' or 'inefficient,' your subconscious now allows you to communicate in levels of efficiency! So if you disagree with something, refer to it as inefficient. This will make it easier to see new and more efficient ideas.

Remember that words are extremely powerful, Consider if you were to stop yourself from using the word 'BUT' and every time replace it with the word 'AND'. Simply never saying 'BUT' again will assist in finding ways to express your thoughts in a positive way.

Can you feel the difference in these two sentences?

"But what if......"

"And what if....."

The powerful intention behind using the word 'AND' instead of 'BUT' will have an amazing impact on your positivity. This mental shift in thinking will create a subconscious system of letting thoughts, feelings and ideas take their natural cycle.

Similarly, if you forget words with self- imposed limitations such as, would, could, should, try, hope, etc. they will no longer have power over you, or control your time and desires. Instead, if you think you've failed, try 'next time' or if you feel you are unable to do something, use the word 'yet'.

"I'm not able to climb that mountain, yet."

The World Is What You Think It Is

Everything around you is there on its own merit, with its own purpose, and will continue to exist without you ever even being aware of it. Because of this, facts are merely your observations and interpretations of the world around you.

No matter how long an interpretation or belief is held, if a new belief is a more efficient expression of that which you are focusing on, the new belief will instantly replace the old view with no inner turmoil or hardship. Re-read that and let it sink in for a minute!

There is no conflict when a previously held belief (in your subconscious) and a desire for change (in your conscious mind) are met with the understanding that the new method is a more effective and efficient method of doing or seeing things.

The most effective and efficient method will always win in the end

You create your own reality based on your beliefs and perceptions.

CHANGE YOUR THINKING

=

CHANGE YOUR PERCEPTION

=

CHANGE YOUR EXPERIENCES

=

CHANGE YOUR WORLD

Your Intention Dictates Your Reality

If your body is sick and you can use self-hypnosis effectively, you can go into your own body as a Doctor would and find out exactly when and where the problem first came up, why it is manifesting, and how the situation can be remedied.

Sometimes the body manifests the secret desires of the subconscious and you are left guessing as to why you keep sabotaging yourself.

It's important to know that your body is controlled by your mind and your mind is under direct control from your will. So focus on what you want to change, and watch as your new purpose directs your mind and body to change or behave in the way you desire.

Before you agree to do anything that might add even the smallest amount of stress to your life, ask yourself, 'What is my truest intention?' Give yourself time to let a 'Yes' resound within you. When it's right, I guarantee that your entire body will feel it.

~ Oprah Winfrey

Personal Mastery Exercises For Intention & Desire

1. If you knew you couldn't fail, list 3 projects you would embark on right now. What would need to be different in your life for these to come true?

******

2. Spend a minute and identify 3 of the most successful personal moments of your life, your crowning accomplishments. Now list 3 things you would like to have written on your headstone to epitomize your life.

How can you use this example for living your life to its fullest?

******

3. Creativity is the mental manipulation of past experiences into a new or different way of doing something. Find 3 things you'd do if you knew you only had 6 months to live. Now flip it and find 3 things you would do if you just won $10 million.

******

4. Name 3 of the most important values to you. Are they in sync with 3 of your most important goals in life?

Can you combine this with the 3 activities that give you the greatest feelings of fulfillment?

True happiness awaits if you can.

Specialized Routine To Increase Intention & Desire

1. ENERGY ASSESSMENT DRILL
On your tracksheet, rate the overall level of current Intention and Desire. Quantify your expectations and experiences numerically - RIGHT THIS MINUTE.

2. BIOFEEDBACK BREATHING EXERCISE
After finding your pulse, synchronize with your breathing in a 3 beats system. A full inhale takes 3 full beats of your heart, then hold for 3 beats, then exhale for 3 beats and again hold for 3 beats while your lungs are empty. Complete this cycle 3 times for 3 full breathes. Think; in for 3 - hold for 3 - out for 3 - hold for 3.

3. BLACKBOARD HI-LITE DRILL
Write your goal on a blackboard or whiteboard, or use paper or visualize. Write out R - E - L - A - X - then erase it backwards, i.e. erase the letter X first. Breathe fully between each letter that you write or erase.

4. SUCCESS VAULT EXERCISE
When in your private mental room, find your Success Vault with all the recorded peak performance moments of your life. Use a copy of your goal, if you've accomplished it before, or find a new visual for a reference if you are using a new goal.

5. INTENSE MEMORY RECALL DRILL

Find a memory of your goal, or create a parallel experience from which you draw from. Take this memory from your Success Vault and replace any old ones with newer versions.

6. PRE-PERFORMANCE VISUALIZATION

See yourself from within your own body as you actualize your goal from the 1st person point of view.

7. POST-PERFORMANCE VISUALIZATION

See yourself on a giant TV from a 3rd person point of view, as you watch and correct any flaws that you see in yourself while actualizing your goal.

INTENSITY

The Principles of Intensity & Power

A Case Study

I had a very powerful and unique experience with one of my clients that personally helped me to reach new levels of self-hypnosis and belief, that I wouldn't have felt were logically possible for me, had I not worked with this person.

She came to me with a giant cyst on her elbow. She explained that it had just 'appeared out of nowhere,' and within a few days was about an inch high, and then within a couple of weeks it had become $2\frac{1}{2}$ inches high, wide and round, like a small ping pong ball was about to burst out of her elbow.

She was, of course, extremely concerned about it. Her level of fearful intensity and focus caused her to go to a dark, restrictive place, where there was no abundance, and there was no love. She sought medical attention and was told surgery was the only option, but her fear increased around that too, as having someone cut it out could not guarantee that it would never resurface again.

My client was a very fast-paced person, tightly wound and a little uptight. I felt she needed to relax and smile more and to take control of her vibrational frequency and emotional activation levels. She was always running at 8 or 9 out of 10, no matter what the situation was, and as we worked together, she began to understand when to be calm or where her intensity was needed, and how to activate each one for the best outcome of any situation.

After several sessions, she was able to understand that she had been shining a spotlight on all of her worries and fears, and that intensity had been multiplying and expanding those fears, adding fuel to the fire. She came to realize she could let go of her worry and completely flip that intensity and focus onto the positive rather than the negative. In one of her visualizations, she took off her skin, washed it in the golden river of healing waters, and when she put her skin back on, noticed that the cyst was no longer there.

In that moment, she felt abundant, expansive and happy and believed that the cyst was no longer a problem. It had, after all come from nowhere, no-one had injected it into her, and she would have it leave her in the same way it had arrived.

She began by internally figuring out what had caused it, making peace with it, and physically watching and reaffirming every day, as the cyst got smaller and smaller.

And so, over the space of several sessions she was able to bring that cyst down to only a bump. Her medical team were astounded and her surgery was postponed.

Years later, she's knows it will never happen again, because she understands that worry and fear, logical or not, justified or not, is an incredibly intense, focused spotlight, and if she shines that on negativity, the fear and the terror will catch on fire and consume her.

If instead she shines that intensity spotlight on the positive, exclusively to the elimination of all else, there is no room for anything else. Light is so much more powerful than darkness.

For me, watching this unfold was a clear example of how the mind and body are connected. By looking at yourself in a whole new way and understanding your relationship to your body, you can be aware of how the mind can trigger a physical reaction in the body.

Single-minded focus and intensity can, and does, make physical changes in the body every day.

All Power Comes From Within

No one has any power, control or influence over you, or anything in your life, unless you first decide to let them!

Because there is no real separation between you, your body, your mind or anything around you, all separation is nothing more than an illusion for labeling and categorizing experiences and events.

For us to understand and remember different experiences, we must first separate them. The system you currently use to separate experiences is exactly the same system that was taught to you as an infant, and it is still running the show.

Update your internal belief system with what you find to be congruent in how you want to live your life now, as an adult.

If you change the way you view complications and conflicts, they will cease to be

When you encounter a problem, first try to TRANSFER it, perhaps to someone more qualified to deal with it. You can also ELIMINATE seeing the issue as a problem. Or finally, you can ACCEPT the situation as it is and look to gain new insight in how to deal with it.

Now Is The Moment Of Power

You are not bound by any experience in the past, nor by any perception of the future. You have the power in the present moment to change limiting beliefs and consciously plant seeds for the future.

Your future is what you choose it to be. You are free to whatever degree you realize this and act upon it!

FEAR ~
Nothing More Than A Belief In A 'False Education Appearing Real'

By knowing and understanding this basic rule, you can empower yourself and know that you choose your beliefs. Self-limiting doubts and beliefs no longer need to exist. When you update your old education with a new perception, self-limiting beliefs are replaced by new positive and powerful beliefs.

Basic Rules Of Subconscious Modification Programming

The subconscious mind is easily trained. If an event is repeated for 21-30 days and/or nights in a row, and your conscious attention is focused on it, this action will automatically become a habit.

Because the subconscious mind is not a vacuum, any new or more efficient method of doing something, that is a new habit, will replace any previously existing habit that is less efficient.

Whether or not the conscious mind approves, the programming of the subconscious will automatically accept anything that has attention focused on it for long enough.

Change will happen automatically and without conscious awareness

The last thing that you consciously focus on before you sleep will be continually replayed over and over in your subconscious throughout the night.

If you listen to Audio at night as you fall asleep, you can, by no conscious effort or will, reprogram any part of your personality, or even learn a new language!

Direct suggestion works as you fall asleep and can happen in as little as 30 days!

Personal Mastery Exercises For Intensity & Power

1. You know that the harder you concentrate on something, the more of it and only it you see, until it fills you, and you can see nothing else but that thing. This is perfect if you need to focus on something like a physical task or "zoom-in" to isolate a problem.

To solve a problem, "click" your mental camera's zoom back a few levels of perception. Turn off your mental "zoom-in" feature and sense the bigger picture to create links and relationships between groups of ideas and images. Learn to zoom in and zoom out in order to see the whole picture on several levels before you act.

******

2. Practice your "energy assessment drill" as the "urge control meter" technique with 3 things that are beyond your control right now. They can range from food to sex and everything in between.

Find ways to change their impact on you. Numerically, lower their power over you, by finding negative counterparts to them. (Using the -10 to +10 measuring chart found in your daily tracksheets)

For example, love pizza (a 9 out of 10 on the chart) and can't seem to shake the desire, day or night? Try thinking about cold pizza (4/10) or all the toppings you hate (0/10) or 3 day old pizza (-3/10) left out in the sun (-9/10), until the urge is under your control.

******

3. Develop 3 anchors that you can use to flip the emotional state you're in. Now pick 3 physical triggers that you can use everyday, anywhere. Your anchor might be the face of your child, and if triggered by bending and flexing the index finger of your right hand 5 times, this might be used to regain your composure if angered, scared or hurt.

******

4. Find 3 fears that have limited you in the past, based on them appearing as real. If you already conquered them in the past, write how you found the truth and then used it to break the F.E.A.R.

If you still live with them, then pick 3 triggers you can use to break them and how you will use them to destroy your fear.

Specialized Routine To Increase Intensity & Power

1. ENERGY ASSESSMENT DRILL
On your tracksheet, rate the overall level of current Intensity and Power. Quantify your expectations and experiences numerically.

2. CENTERING DRILL
With a straight body, bend forward and backward in increasingly smaller arcs while maintaining balance. Then move side to side until perfectly centered. Maintain this balanced state for several breaths, then test each direction by holding your balance for 10 seconds at each extreme end.

3. CONCENTRATED BREATHING EXERCISE
Any movements you make are interchangeable, focus instead on the tension in every possible body part and ensure that every movement is accompanied by an in or out breath. Follow a basic formula to create your own exercise by first, focusing on the dynamic tension felt throughout every part of your body. Then add the act of breathing in accord with every movement, either in or out. Finally, and for your purposes here, comes the actual movements which, if you follow the first two rules are not that important. Go slow, breathe and tense every muscle in your body while moving.

4. MENTAL SCREAM DRILL

With each breath focus a ball of negative emotions and energy in your stomach area, and let it get tighter and tighter. Now let it explode while you scream silently in your mind. Ensure dynamic tension throughout your body (squeeze all your muscles) while you scream, take breaths and continue for as long as you need, then stop both simultaneously – when you no longer feel the initial stress.

5. TARGETING DRILL

Choose any characteristic that you wish to improve on or develop and create a complete change of state by giving yourself a physical trigger to enter and exit that state. Visualize an arrow to carry your new goal to its bulls-eye. Start by using any exercise that puts you into a quiet, powerful state of mind and body, like Biofeedback breathing for example. Then create a trigger (like squeezing your left fist 5 times), that puts you into the archery range. Now see your goal as your target, adjust your aim accordingly and see what it will take for you to reach your goal.

Reflection ~

VODKA Vs. WATER

There was a time in my life, while I was working as a Medical Hypnotherapist, when I needed a little extra income. I was struggling to pay the bills and make rent, so I decided to moonlight as a stage hypnotherapist.

I wanted to put on a show that would showcase some mental training skills and exercises of the mind, rather than to make people 'cluck like a duck or bark like a chicken,' and stuff like that.

I took a look at a few principles and considered the difference between Vodka and water, and the interaction both have on the body. If you were to ask an actor to drink some water and pretend that it's Vodka, honestly, it would take some of the best actors on the planet to truly convince someone they were drinking Vodka when it was water.

However, with the right mental persuasion, I was able to convince the audience that they were drinking delicious, quenching, simple water, when in fact it was Vodka, and vice versa.

The very interesting part of all this though, was those that believed they were drinking water, when it was actually Vodka, experienced no cognitive impairment as would be expected when drinking that amount of Vodka. They would go on to perform other tasks and demonstrate no change in their cognitive or physical appearance. They truly believed they were drinking water.

Those that drank water, however, when believing they were drinking Vodka, would perform in a way that you would expect when someone had drunk a large amount of Vodka. The mind's eye will absolutely believe what it perceives and believes is happening in any given moment.

With mental training you can be more aware of what is really happening 'right now' compared to what you believe.

That's the absolute edge and power of where mental training can take you.

PRODUCTIVITY

The Principles of Productivity & Energy

A Case Study

I remember a very special case where a wonderful young lady came to see me. I had been working with an Olympic gymnastic association and she heard I was in Fredericton, New Brunswick. She booked an entire day of therapy with me, before I flew home, and being a paraplegic, without feeling below the waist, had driven her hand-control car for over eight hours all the way from St. John's, Newfoundland, just to see me!

The intention for the session was to try and get to the source of her trauma, so she could let go of the extreme pain that she connected with the accident that had left her paralyzed.

She was an amazing, happy and positive young woman in her mid-late twenties, ready to take on the world, yet believed she was experiencing a hindrance to her energy levels, desire, focus and productivity. Every time an issue came close to the area of her trauma, no matter where she was and what mood she was in, her productivity would be instantly squashed.

As she told me her story, it touched my heart the way it would anyone's. She was on her way home from college to visit her family for Christmas, sitting in the back of a car with a lap belt on, when a drunk driver swerved and hit the car head-on at 100mph. She literally bent in half, snapping her vertebrae 2-up from her coccyx.

When she was describing the events of her accident, and in detail, her rehabilitation, I asked her if there were any highlights. Her face lit up when she began talking about her husband, and I expressed how heart-warming it was that her husband had stood by her during her rehab, as I know a lot of guys wouldn't be able to handle it.

"Oh no, you've got the wrong idea," she said. "It was quite the opposite. He never knew me when I could walk, he never knew me as a Varsity volleyball player, he only met me when I was paralyzed."

My heart exploded, my tears overflowed, and I was stunned by the beauty of that love. I knew that would be the anchor we could use to create triggers for her to overcome and let go of her pain.

When we began therapy, using standard reframing NLP techniques, I noticed right away that she was sitting back passively, watching her accident happen, as if in the audience at a movie theatre.

I realized that we could somehow reframe it for her by watching it over and over again, with different types of music; clown music, happy music, scary music. At some point the trauma stops having an impact, it stops having a hold on you, releases it's grip and allows you to let go.

It was one of the longest sessions I've ever facilitated. If you've ever done this type of work, you'll understand that 12 hours is a lifetime. It was incredibly powerful and emotional, and she was crying throughout the therapy. We only stopped a couple of times to eat and go to the bathroom, and the compounding effect of going back into flow would put her into a deeper state of trance. With this type of therapy, every time you go out, you go back in easier, quicker, and deeper.

Towards the end of the day, while we were re-visualizing this traumatic event, going back over it again and again, I saw her left foot start to flap, moving rapidly forward and back. I looked at her eyes. They were closed, but the REM was going back and forth like crazy.

Of course, I don't know what she was seeing or visualizing, but her foot was panicking. Before seeing her, I'd read about some of the physical reactions that could happen in these situations without the person who is paralyzed knowing about it, or having any control over it. This implies that there would be no awareness for her, similar to when you roll over when you're sleeping, but you have no awareness of it.

However, when we finished the incredibly emotional, uplifting, yet draining day, she asked, "Did you touch me at any point during therapy?"

I couldn't hold back the look of shock on my face. She may as well have asked me if I was a pink dinosaur! "I was sitting in the chair on the other side of the room, and you were on the bed. I was about 15ft away at all times," I said, but then I challenged her, "hang on, are you saying that you 'felt' that I touched you?"

"Well yes!" she laughed. "At one point about 30-40 minutes ago, I was aware of a sensation as if you were touching my left foot, maybe squeezing it, or supporting it."

"Not even close," I said, "but if I had touched your foot, how could you possibly feel that? Your eyes were closed. There's definitely something physical going on. You need to get to a doctor or rehab, work out what's happening, and maybe get yourself back to walking!"

The look of surprise and gratitude on her face was amazing, and I could tell she was letting go of some trauma in that moment.

"Look at it this way," I said, "If I did physically touch you, the fact that you could feel me, with your eyes closed, means you could feel 'something', and if you feel it in your body, then you can heal. And let's say I didn't touch you, but in your mind, you thought I did, you were so convinced of that thought that you genuinely felt something happening in your foot. Either way, you need to get back into therapy and heal yourself because there is something going on mentally and you're ready to make that mind-body connection."

"How do you know all this?" she asked.

"Well, about 30 minutes ago I watched your foot flap like an uncontrollable seal flapping to get a fish," I laughed, so excited about her possibilities. "You've got some work to do! Get your butt back into rehab and see what you can achieve!"

That possibility had the most incredible impact on her productivity. When she truly let go of the pain, her energy skyrocketed.

She's been in contact many times over the years and she continues to work through rehab, challenging her condition and improving everyday. She's progressed tremendously since we first met, all those years ago.

It's a spectacular success story. A remarkable story of the power of human hope and spirit, and what you can do with your energy when you direct and focus to one ultimate goal.

The Energy Of Your Body Is Totally Controlled By The Intention Of Your Mind

If you are in a positive, resourceful state, no amount of negativity can get through to you. It's as if you have a sphere of white light in a big bubble all around you, shielding you from negativity.

You can have this resourceful, energized state anytime you want!

If you want to summon up physical strength, courage or a non-critical, non-analyzing part of your mind, the subconscious is the most effective tool you can use.

Before any moment of potential stress, either positive or negative, breathe deeply at least three times and concentrate on a mental image of yourself, an image of what you are striving to become, your highest you. This image will project outward and relax your body, while sharpening your mind.

You are as tired, hungry, sad OR happy and healthy as you THINK you are!

By changing your view of the outside world, you can also now change your view of your inside world, including your body, and your current mental, physical and spiritual state of health.

Your Energy Flows Where Your Attention Goes

When you direct your energy subconsciously onto a thought or feeling, this forms a blueprint in your mind, which then will create the nearest physical equivalent to those thoughts and feelings in your life.

The more points of reference you create, the farther out of your paradigm you can go and safely return

Use everything you have EVER done, successfully or unsuccessfully as a point of reference. It is a springboard of experience that you can launch yourself from. NEVER FEAR! You can always go back to the last level of experience, except now it is not as significant and not as magically unattainable as it may once have been.

Your greatest success is simply your latest experience, becoming the bare minimum for what you can now accomplish, no longer the pinnacle of what you once were.

The Process of Manifestation
- explains how you create your reality

1. The conscious mind focuses on something - a thought, feeling or event.

2. The subconscious mind treats the focus of attention as an event and records it in memory.

3. The Super-conscious mind uses the memory as a pattern or blueprint to create an equivalent physical experience.

Ask for what you want,

and be prepared to get it!

~ Maya Angelou

Every Day Morning Routine To Increase Productivity and Boost Immunity

1. Pray or practice Gratitude.
Be thankful for all the miracles that surround you.

2. Millionaire mindset incantation.
Only use words that create an emotional response within you.

3. Martial Arts practice.

4. Learn something new.
Watch a video or listen to a podcast from someone you've not interacted with before. Or find a topic that fascinates you, yet you know very little about. 10 minutes of learning something new can have an amazing impact on your day.

5. Express kindness and spend quality time with your family and those that mean the most to you.

BONUS

6. Smile.
Choose to smile, laugh and have fun.

What an incredible day ahead you will have!

Personal Mastery Exercises For Productivity & Energy

List 3 words that are no longer usfeul. You can forget these words altogther - forever.

******

Find 3 differences in belief that you have with your parents.

Remember their belief system is the same one you were originally programmed with since childhood. It's a belief system you have greatly expanded on, and evolved. The same is true of the current system of belief that you hold to be true now. It is changeable, updateable, molded every time you make life changes. Like today.

******

Find 3 major improvements to the differences of belief you have with your parents, beliefs that hold true today.

******

Find 3 words that are limiting you and that you wish to replace with positive words.

Find the "good" root of these words; find what they "really" are trying to say or do or make you feel, and switch them with replacements that are conducive to your new beliefs.

******

Tension, either in the mind or body, is a "do-it-yourself" project.

Find 3 ways that you are personally contributing to the amount of stress in your life and see if you wish to pay the price for it.

Specialized Routine To Increase Productivity & Energy

1. ENERGY ASSESSMENT DRILL
On your tracksheet, rate the overall level of current Productivity and Energy. Quantify your expectations and experiences numerically,

2. FACIAL SELF-MASSAGE EXERCISE
Beginning at the top of the front of the head, make circular motions with the fingers and heel of the hand. Cover the ears, all major bones in the head all the way around, from the neck up and the sinuses. Stop when your breathing is deeper and fuller and when your face is tingling and feels revived.

3. BIOFEEDBACK BREATHING EXERCISE
After finding your pulse, synchronize with your breathing in a 3 beats system. A full inhale takes 3 full beats of your heart, then hold for 3 beats, then exhale for 3 beats and again hold for 3 beats while your lungs are empty. Complete this cycle 3x for 3 full breathes. Think in for 3 - hold for 3 - out for 3 - hold for 3.

4. INNER BODY VISUALIZATION
Let your eyes look through your skull as if it were made of glass. As they leave your head, let them look at your body on the inside as they go through every part of you, from head to toe, and check to see that everything inside is operating well and everything is a

light, healthy pink color. Let your eyes shoot out a healing white laser beam at any body part that is not a healthy, light pink color. When everything looks fine, send the eyes back to their place and look through the glass skull again.

5. RANDOM ESCAPE VISUALIZATION

Start off by seeing yourself in a deep lush jungle with a huge tree in the middle of a clearing. Look up the tree to a branch where you see an eagle resting. Count to 3 and become that eagle. Now fly high over a mountain-top tree, fly over the ocean then dive into the sea, as you become a flying fish and you swim/fly through the ocean. You make your way back to land and end up on the same beach you came from. As you fly out of the water, count to 3 and become a panther. Now run as that panther through the bush to the very tree where you started. Run up it onto your old branch and count to 3 and turn back into the eagle. Now rest on your perch, awaiting you next flight.

Reflection ~

MIXED MARTIAL ARTS

There is an incredibly powerful and extremely well respected lady named Daria Albers who is famous in the MMA community. As a mixed martial artist, she has been renowned for the last 20 years as one of the greatest striking athletes in MMA history.

She works with all the top names from McGregor to Israel and everybody in between. Besides being an incredible striker and an incredible striking coach, her magical skill is her ability to incorporate her background and bachelors degree in psychology to help athletes discover their own magical powers and how to attain them in a minimal period of time.

When training elite athletes, sports psychologists and mental training specialists use a training regimen called ADA - standing for, associated / disassociated / associated. (First Person / Third Person / First Person)

Using this methodology, the athlete will firstly focus on their body or performance in an associated way (A). They will see it in first person, through their own eyes. Next they will observe their actions in a dissociated way (D), completely disconnected, as if watching in third person on a big screen in front of them, or as if a drone is flying overhead. Lastly, they will see themselves again in an associated way (A), through their own eyes in first person, but this time their performance is improved and enhanced.

Coming from the Netherlands, Daria follows a different mental training regimen. She uses DAD - disassociated / associated / disassociated. (Third Person / First Person / Third Person)

I find this really fascinating, as for almost 30 years in

North America, we've been doing it the exact opposite way. It's so very radically different with a completely different recipe, but what is strikingly fascinating is that while Daria and I use opposite methodologies, both of us achieve the same beneficial and impactful results.

The end result is the same and produces champions no matter what process is used. These mental training practices give athletes a cutting edge to understand inside and outside their body, and to slow down time and perception so they can achieve exceptional levels of peak performance.

Checklist For Success

1. DAILY TRACKSHEETS
Day-by-day benchmarks to track your success and highlight instantly, areas for immediate improvement.
Done daily

2. N.M.S. POWER NIGHT-TIME MANTRA SYSTEM GOAL CARDS
Night-time Mantra System Power Goal Cards let you clearly visualize your goal in the present tense and ensure that you can duplicate your success with other future goals.
Done nightly and as needed daily

3. PERSONAL MASTERY EXERCISES
Private and deeply personal reflections of intensely powerful moments and themes in your life.
Done once

4. ESSENTIAL PRINCIPLES
The heart and soul of the program, separated into 3 sections INTENTION / INTENSITY / PRODUCTIVITY providing inspirations and incantations for life-long change.
Done once

5. MENTAL, PHYSICAL AND EMOTIONAL DRILLS
Broken down into specialized segments to let you quickly and easily access the exact exercise or routine that you need.
Do this daily in routines as needed

6. CHRONICLES OF CHANGE - 30 DAY SUCCESS JOURNAL

A 30 day journal has places that let you express the little changes that happen to you day-by-day, places to jot-down anything special that happens to you during your change that doesn't seem to fit in anywhere else, spots where you can classify the causes and affects, the low and highpoints of each day, track your progress and make assessments every week of your change.

Use Everyday

7. PERSONAL STRESS QUIZ & WORKLOAD STRESS QUIZ

Pinpoint the source of stress in your daily life with these two quizzes designed to let you identify and isolate that which causes you the most stress - whether at work, rest or play.

Complete before and after the program to check progress

N.M.S. (Night-Time Mantra System) and Power Goal Card Selection

This is a non-passive component of your change. You won't be able to just read something or listen to something in this part. Here, you'll have to write out something very special. There are certain words that when written down and spoken aloud with conviction generate a kind of electrical power that radiates up and down your spine and outward to your fingers and toes. Some cultures call this a 'quickening'. During this time, you are open to receive suggestions directly into your subconscious, and that is why it is so important that you choose words that best describe the future you that you are striving to be.

Words spoken to better your mood are sometimes called affirmations, things like;

"Today is a great day, I will not let anything ruin my day. I am in control - so watch out!"

These sayings, unfortunately rarely hold any sway over us, and if any, their affects are temporary at best

Instead, what we are creating here is more of an incantation, words spoken with intent to invoke power. N.M.S. Goal Cards must be written in the present tense and with no negative words or imagery, as if you are experiencing the new you right now and are describing how it feels. This has the most psychological impact.

Try this: say the above affirmation out loud and see if you feel silly afterwards or strong and empowered. If we use words that mean something to us and pull on our heartstrings, then we use emotional fuel to help the change take place for life. If you use the name of a loved one and swear on their life that you'll quit smoking, you might be setting yourself up for a failure and some hard feelings. That's why your message to yourself in your N.M.S. Goal Card has to be stated in the present and positively.

For example, lets convert the above affirmation into a proper incantation;
"Today, like all my days, is a great day. I am in control of all I can be and in (my children's name) strive to be even better as I continue to improve each day."

Now add your personal reason for your change and how it will feel once you've accomplished it, and you have the beginnings of a proper N.M.S. Goal Card. This card is one of the cornerstones of the program and is integral to your change for life. Read your card out loud throughout the day whenever you need a reminder or to get yourself back on track. i.e. If a smoking craving hits you at 2:30pm - read your N.M.S. Goal Card out loud several times to center yourself. Carry your card with you at all times.

The key is to read your N.M.S. Goal Card right before you go to bed at night

This is because the mind focuses on the last thing it encounters before bed and cycles this thought pattern, round and round, all night long.

This explains why your sleep will be more restless if you watch the news before bed, and you'll wake up in a slightly sour mood. You can record your mantra on your mobile device and listen to it before sleeping, as well as saying it out loud, so that you'll think about your N.M.S. Goal Card all night long and reinforce the suggestions.

Unless you use your own words, your N.M.S. Goal Card has NO POWER

If you're trying to lose weight you can use certain parts of this incantation for your N.M.S. Goal Card.
"I love my life, I have absolute control over my eating habits, I love my body and the way it moves, I feel strong and healthy and want to be even more so."

For smokers -
"I breathe freely and deeply and am strong and healthy. My lungs are clear and I am in complete control of anything that I put into my lungs. I choose fresh clear air as my lungs get cleaner and stronger."

You'll know that your N.M.S. Goal Card is finished when it invokes an emotional response from you after reading it. If it doesn't affect you, then it's not the ultra-personal message to yourself that it needs to be.

When you've written your N.M.S. Goal Card and it causes a 'quickening' in you, then you can move on

Reflection ~

My Mom.
I have a couple of amazing examples from my mom's life experiences that showcase what the mind can achieve, and the power of self-hypnosis when fully focused.

When she emigrated from Russia to Canada, she had 18 gold teeth. Somehow she convinced her dental surgeon to allow the removal and repair of these teeth without anesthetic. She was able to perform 'hypno-dontics' on herself, going into a state of trance for her pain relief. She requested the dentist gave her a verbal cue, or a slight tap on her finger when he was about to start a painful part of the procedure. She was able to drop into a deeper state of trance at this time. Also, during the process, there would normally be a significant amount of blood loss however, my mom was able to visualize a dry desert, and the dentist, and the students he had brought in to watch the procedure, were baffled by how little blood was visible. It was a 3 hour surgery and extraction and yet the following day, my mom was able to talk to the dentist and let him know she was feeling ok! He was amazed. He expected her mouth to be so swollen that talking would be impossible, but she experienced minimal bleeding and discomfort.

This mental training and mind control stood her in good stead throughout her life, but particularly in her sixties when it possibly saved her life! It was an accident that could happen to anyone. She was barefoot in the kitchen, and reaching to get a plate, when she dropped it and it fell to the floor shattering into hundreds of pieces. One 'giant' shard jumped up and hit her in the front of the foot, just above the ankle. At this point she was 'spurting' blood and the cut was so deep all the ligaments and anatomy underneath could be seen! She was in control of her emotions and calm enough to call an ambulance, as well as me, as she knew I had some basic EMT training. The ambulance staff were able to control the bleeding, but Mom needed to go to the hospital and I went along with her. She was able to use self-hypnosis while the doctor repaired the ligaments and nerves that were damaged, without anesthetic.

The following year, Mom was diagnosed with Ovarian Cancer. She used her mental training principles and techniques to remain calm and relaxed during the whole experience, including surgery and removal of 5 organs. She reminded herself to feel powerful, before and after surgery. She didn't allow herself to feel any negativity. She went within and was able to go the extra mile to become a cancer survivor, with no remissions years later.

She's an incredible lady and has been an amazing inspiration throughout my life and to this day, teaching me mind over reality and mind over matter in a very meaningful way.

Epilogue

I was invited to join a cool Mastermind session with some high-end, talented performance coaches. The group consisted of people with varying amounts of experience in the coaching field. Some, like me, had decades working with elite athletes, CEO's and peak performers, while others had been coaching for 4-5 years, and a couple were only recently qualified with just 4-6 months experience.

After some discussions around mindset and performance, one of the newer coaches, asked an interesting question. "Why is it that I'm at a point where I know I've had some success, but I'm just not feeling abundance? I understand what I'm doing, I'm progressing and have some happiness, but I don't seem to be able to come from a place of abundance like you guys."

A couple of coaches came back with some ideas. One suggested he should get 'busy', get so busy that everything becomes a blur. The busy-ness would make him feel full, and because of that fullness, abundance would follow.

I'm OK with that concept, but it feels like a very taxing way to go, and maybe not the most elegant solution, so I chimed in. "If I was to coach you, I would make this a lot easier for you. It sounds like you're putting a lot of work on your shoulders, and if it doesn't live up to your expectations 100% then it's not working. But there is an easier way. What if you had the mindset that abundance is equal to 'something'? In this way, if you have that 'something', you must by definition have abundance. You could almost reverse engineer it that way."

Well, now he was on the edge of his seat. "What is it? How does it work?" he asked. "What equals abundance?"

"It's very, very easy," I said. "Gratitude equals Abundance. Think about it. Once you start progressing, challenging yourself and overcoming those challenges, you can't help but be happy. Once you start feeling happy, you can't help but count your blessings and feel grateful for the things that make you happy. And if you are grateful, every little bit of gratitude you express will help you feel more abundant."

I'd like to suggest here, that you start counting your blessings, literally and figuratively. Wake up and appreciate that you actually did 'wake up'. Be grateful that you can breathe on your own, walk on your own, and think clearly. It is an incredible plethora of blessings that we have bestowed upon us, every moment of every day. It is so incredible and insurmountably uncountable, like grains of sand or drops of water in the ocean.

Gratitude by itself is the most incredible, most powerful emotion, like hope and love mixed together. Gratitude when you are feeling it 'properly' is vibrating on an energetic frequency, at it's unique megahertz and allowing whatever comes out of you to radiate positivity. With that expression, you can't help but feel grateful and abundant at the same time.

The interesting thing about 'Gratitude Equals Abundance' is that it's not a two way street. That's how you know it's real. These two things are not automatically interchangeable, nothing is. There are many opulent and incredibly bestowed and blessed people who feel abundance all around them. It self perpetuates and makes them want more. It doesn't automatically make them feel grateful. While gratitude always equals abundance, abundance does not necessarily equal gratitude.

The easiest and simplest way to be aligned and move through life with the least amount of resistance is to remind yourself that genuinely feeling grateful is something you can feel automatically, and in turn you will feel abundant. And if you do ever happen to find yourself in a moment of pure abundance, remind yourself to be grateful! But start with gratitude, right now.

My new friend was touched and happy after our conversation. There are always novel, complicated and scientific ways to find solutions to that which we are curious about, but often, it's the simple ideas that can really shift a paradigm and leave a lasting impression to explore the possibilities of change.

I wish you the absolute best in your change and many more to come.

Good for you and good on you - and good for all of us, as your transformation serves everyone. Every growth or expansion affects the universe in a positive way. And remember, everyone is a universe unto themselves.

I wish you all the most abundance, gratitude, and happiness and to never stop progressing and growing.

'Our deepest fear is not that we are inadequate.
Our deepest fear is that we are
powerful beyond measure.
It is our light, not our darkness
that most frightens us.
We ask ourselves, "Who am I to be brilliant,
gorgeous, talented, fabulous?"
Actually, who are you not to be?
You are a child of God.
Your playing small does not serve the world.
There is nothing enlightened about shrinking
so other people won't feel insecure around you.
We are all meant to shine, as children do.
We were born to make manifest the glory
of God that is within us.
It's not just in some of us; it's in everyone.
And as we let our own light shine, we unconsciously
give other people permission
to do the same.
As we are liberated from our own fear, our presence
automatically liberates others.'

~ Marianne Williamson

RESOURCES

Stress Quiz
Workplace Quiz
Daily Tracksheets
30 Day Success Journal

STRESS QUIZ

Answer these 12 questions honestly to see where stress is affecting you in your life!

Scoring: constantly = 4 / frequently = 3 / sometimes = 2 / rarely = 1 / never = 0

1. I get sudden feelings of fear and panic _____
2. I am troubled by difficulty getting to sleep, staying asleep or waking early _____
3. I feel irritable, edgy and bad tempered _____
4. I have irregular eating patterns and either eat too much or too little _____
5. I smoke or drink too much or take tranquilizers or other drugs _____
6. I suffer from upset stomach, diarrhea or constipation _____
7. I feel exhausted and tired _____
8. I can't turn off certain worrying thoughts _____
9. I get headaches or migraines _____
10. I am obsessive about certain issues such as illness, cleanliness, or food _____
11. I feel physically run down _____
12. I put off seeing friends and have no interest in hobbies _____

TOTAL _____

How did you score?

46 POINTS OR MORE
Obviously you are stressed. You are walking a path to many pathological illnesses that could be too numerous to list here. Consider everything from a job change to lifestyle modification. There is far too much stress in your life. You really have no choice but to change your life and your stress levels, before your doctor intervenes.

36 - 45 POINTS
There is way too much stress in your life to ignore the warning signs. Health complications are just around the corner if you don't work on getting a sense of balance in your life. Too much of anything – work, relationships, drugs, etc. – cause high levels of stress. It's time to bring the stress in your life down before it affects your health. Any work you do to lower your stress will immediately make a difference in your life.

24 - 35 POINTS
You are in the middle ground in terms of stress levels. One more event in your life that causes stress will be enough to put you over the edge and bring you into another category of risk. However, one less event (if you can diminish any area of stress in your life), will bring you into a healthy balance and let you remain productive while not letting your life get the better of you and run you, instead of the other way around.

13 - 23 POINTS

Stress is balanced and you are in control of the majority of emergencies that arise. If you learn to cope even more effectively, you will become super-productive and still have the strength to smile at the end of the day. However, if you take on too many extra tasks, you could suffer the consequences, as too much stress will spread you thin and leave gaps in the activities that you normally could adapt to and perform well. You can learn to get even better at balancing your stress.

12 or LESS POINTS

You are a superstar. You have learned to channel all the crap in your life into positive, productive results to the best of your abilities, without energy wasted on the outcome. If you were in the above categories, you would worry a lot more than you do now, and as a result would try and alleviate some of that by being more and more productive and thus, more stressed. Focus your efforts on improving your already formidable skills at stress reduction, and then slowly take on more.

WORKPLACE QUIZ

Rate & Rank your level of stress with each
of these questions

Scoring : high stress = 3 / moderate stress = 2 / low stress = 1 / no stress = 0

1. I have too much work to do   _____

2. There are too many roles to play   _____

3. Responsible for managing others   _____

4. My relationship with others at work   _____

5. My salary / wages   _____

6. Continuing to work at home   _____

7. Working long or unsociable hours   _____

8. Unclear what is expected of me   _____

9. Having to make decisions or plans   _____

10. My relationship with my manager   _____

11. Doing a job that does not challenge me   _____

12. Difficulty switching off at home   _____

13. Too many demands on my time   _____

14. Having a few clear objectives   _____

15. Dealing with conflict   _____

16. Little encouragement or support   _____

17. Career and promotion prospects   _____

18. The demands of work on my home life _____
19. Too little work to do _____
20. Changes in the way i'm asked to work _____
21. Work politics _____
22. Lack of colleagues to confide in _____
23. Unpleasant physical environment _____
24. Prioritizing between work and home _____
25. Time pressures and deadlines _____
26. Lack of variety or stimulation _____
27. Fear of making a mistake _____
28. Poor training and guidelines _____
29. Lack of job satisfaction _____
30. My partner's attitude to my work _____
31. Not having the right skills for the job _____
32. Little feedback about my performance _____
33. Meetings / giving presentations _____
34. The general morale of the workplace _____
35. Job insecurity or threat of layoffs _____
36. Changes outside work - finance / illness etc _____

Now transfer your scores for each of the questions into the table on the following page. This will show you where you need to focus your attention in the different areas of your life.

A   B   C   D   E   F

1____ 2____ 3____ 4____ 5____ 6____

7____ 8____ 9____ 10____ 11____ 12____

13____ 14____ 15____ 16____ 17____ 18____

19____ 20____ 21____ 22____ 23____ 24____

25____ 26____ 27____ 28____ 29____ 30____

31____ 32____ 33____ 34____ 35____ 36____

TOTAL:

_____ _____ _____ _____ _____ _____
  A   B   C   D   E   F

How did you score?

A: WORKLOAD

OVER 8
Your workload appears to be creating stress. Seek to make changes in the structure of your job.

BETWEEN 5-8
Your workload is on the verge of being stressful.

BELOW 5
Overload may not be an issue, but a high score for question 19 may indicate that 'underload' is a problem.

B: ROLE

OVER 8
Your job description appears to need clarifying and defining. Confront your manager assertively and make changes.

BETWEEN 5-8
Some clarification is needed regarding your role at work.

BELOW 5
Your role at work does not appear to be a problem.

C: RESPONSIBILITY

OVER 8
You appear to be uncomfortable with your present responsibilities. You may benefit from talking to colleagues who have more experience of responsibility. Ask for more training.

BETWEEN 5-8
You seem to have some difficulties taking responsibility at work.

BELOW 5
You do not appear to have a problem with responsibility.

D: RELATIONSHIPS

OVER 8
Relationships at work appear to be creating stress. Aim to improve the quality of these and seek better support from those around you.

BETWEEN 5-8
Your relationships at work could be a source of stress.

BELOW 5
Relationships at work do not appear to be a problem.

E: JOB SATISFACTION
OVER 8
You appear to have a low level of job satisfaction and possibly do not feel valued at work. Are you doing the right job? Are there more satisfying areas that you could move into?

BETWEEN 5-8
You job could be more satisfying.

BELOW 5
You appear to enjoy your work.

F: HOME / WORK INTERFACE
OVER 8
You seem not to be keeping home and work separate. You may need to re-establish some firm boundaries.

BETWEEN 5-8
Home and work show signs of interacting negatively.

BELOW 5
The interaction between home and work does not appear to be stressful.

DAY # 1

Daily Tracksheet
Success Journal

DAILY TRACKSHEET

6AM - AWAKENING

INTENT/DESIRE   INTENSITY/POWER   PRODUCTIVITY/ENERGY

-10 - 0 - +10 ____   -10 - 0 - +10 ____   -10 - 0 - +10 ____

9AM - ARRIVING AT WORK

INTENT/DESIRE   INTENSITY/POWER   PRODUCTIVITY/ENERGY

-10 - 0 - +10 ____   -10 - 0 - +10 ____   -10 - 0 - +10 ____

1PM - AFTER LUNCH

INTENT/DESIRE   INTENSITY/POWER   PRODUCTIVITY/ENERGY

-10 - 0 - +10 ____   -10 - 0 - +10 ____   -10 - 0 - +10 ____

5PM - WORK DAY END

INTENT/DESIRE   INTENSITY/POWER   PRODUCTIVITY/ENERGY

-10 - 0 - +10 ____   -10 - 0 - +10 ____   -10 - 0 - +10 ____

9PM - BEFORE BED

INTENT/DESIRE   INTENSITY/POWER   PRODUCTIVITY/ENERGY

-10 - 0 - +10 ____   -10 - 0 - +10 ____   -10 - 0 - +10 ____

Chronicles of Change

HIGHS

_____

_____

_____

_____

LOWS

_____

_____

_____

_____

PERSONAL REVELATIONS

DAY # 2

Daily Tracksheet
Success Journal

DAILY TRACKSHEET

6AM - AWAKENING

INTENT/DESIRE   INTENSITY/POWER   PRODUCTIVITY/ENERGY

-10 - 0 - +10 ____   -10 - 0 - +10 ____   -10 - 0 - +10 ____

9AM - ARRIVING AT WORK

INTENT/DESIRE   INTENSITY/POWER   PRODUCTIVITY/ENERGY

-10 - 0 - +10 ____   -10 - 0 - +10 ____   -10 - 0 - +10 ____

1PM - AFTER LUNCH

INTENT/DESIRE   INTENSITY/POWER   PRODUCTIVITY/ENERGY

-10 - 0 - +10 ____   -10 - 0 - +10 ____   -10 - 0 - +10 ____

5PM - WORK DAY END

INTENT/DESIRE   INTENSITY/POWER   PRODUCTIVITY/ENERGY

-10 - 0 - +10 ____   -10 - 0 - +10 ____   -10 - 0 - +10 ____

9PM - BEFORE BED

INTENT/DESIRE   INTENSITY/POWER   PRODUCTIVITY/ENERGY

-10 - 0 - +10 ____   -10 - 0 - +10 ____   -10 - 0 - +10 ____

Chronicles of Change

HIGHS

_____

_____

_____

_____

LOWS

_____

_____

_____

_____

_____

PERSONAL REVELATIONS

DAY # 3

Daily Tracksheet
Success Journal

DAILY TRACKSHEET

6AM - AWAKENING

INTENT/DESIRE   INTENSITY/POWER   PRODUCTIVITY/ENERGY

-10 - 0 - +10 ____   -10 - 0 - +10 ____   -10 - 0 - +10 ____

9AM - ARRIVING AT WORK

INTENT/DESIRE   INTENSITY/POWER   PRODUCTIVITY/ENERGY

-10 - 0 - +10 ____   -10 - 0 - +10 ____   -10 - 0 - +10 ____

1PM - AFTER LUNCH

INTENT/DESIRE   INTENSITY/POWER   PRODUCTIVITY/ENERGY

-10 - 0 - +10 ____   -10 - 0 - +10 ____   -10 - 0 - +10 ____

5PM - WORK DAY END

INTENT/DESIRE   INTENSITY/POWER   PRODUCTIVITY/ENERGY

-10 - 0 - +10 ____   -10 - 0 - +10 ____   -10 - 0 - +10 ____

9PM - BEFORE BED

INTENT/DESIRE   INTENSITY/POWER   PRODUCTIVITY/ENERGY

-10 - 0 - +10 ____   -10 - 0 - +10 ____   -10 - 0 - +10 ____

Chronicles of Change

HIGHS

_____
_____
_____
_____
_____

LOWS

_____
_____
_____
_____
_____

PERSONAL REVELATIONS

DAY # 4

Daily Tracksheet
Success Journal

DAILY TRACKSHEET

6AM - AWAKENING

INTENT/DESIRE   INTENSITY/POWER   PRODUCTIVITY/ENERGY

-10 - 0 - +10 ____   -10 - 0 - +10 ____   -10 - 0 - +10 ____

9AM - ARRIVING AT WORK

INTENT/DESIRE   INTENSITY/POWER   PRODUCTIVITY/ENERGY

-10 - 0 - +10 ____   -10 - 0 - +10 ____   -10 - 0 - +10 ____

1PM - AFTER LUNCH

INTENT/DESIRE   INTENSITY/POWER   PRODUCTIVITY/ENERGY

-10 - 0 - +10 ____   -10 - 0 - +10 ____   -10 - 0 - +10 ____

5PM - WORK DAY END

INTENT/DESIRE   INTENSITY/POWER   PRODUCTIVITY/ENERGY

-10 - 0 - +10 ____   -10 - 0 - +10 ____   -10 - 0 - +10 ____

9PM - BEFORE BED

INTENT/DESIRE   INTENSITY/POWER   PRODUCTIVITY/ENERGY

-10 - 0 - +10 ____   -10 - 0 - +10 ____   -10 - 0 - +10 ____

Chronicles of Change

HIGHS

_____

_____

_____

_____

_____

LOWS

_____

_____

_____

_____

_____

PERSONAL REVELATIONS

DAY # 5

Daily Tracksheet
Success Journal

DAILY TRACKSHEET

6AM - AWAKENING

INTENT/DESIRE   INTENSITY/POWER   PRODUCTIVITY/ENERGY

-10 - 0 - +10 _____   -10 - 0 - +10 _____   -10 - 0 - +10 _____

9AM - ARRIVING AT WORK

INTENT/DESIRE   INTENSITY/POWER   PRODUCTIVITY/ENERGY

-10 - 0 - +10 _____   -10 - 0 - +10 _____   -10 - 0 - +10 _____

1PM - AFTER LUNCH

INTENT/DESIRE   INTENSITY/POWER   PRODUCTIVITY/ENERGY

-10 - 0 - +10 _____   -10 - 0 - +10 _____   -10 - 0 - +10 _____

5PM - WORK DAY END

INTENT/DESIRE   INTENSITY/POWER   PRODUCTIVITY/ENERGY

-10 - 0 - +10 _____   -10 - 0 - +10 _____   -10 - 0 - +10 _____

9PM - BEFORE BED

INTENT/DESIRE   INTENSITY/POWER   PRODUCTIVITY/ENERGY

-10 - 0 - +10 _____   -10 - 0 - +10 _____   -10 - 0 - +10 _____

Chronicles of Change

HIGHS

LOWS

PERSONAL REVELATIONS

DAY # 6

Daily Tracksheet
Success Journal

DAILY TRACKSHEET

6AM - AWAKENING

INTENT/DESIRE   INTENSITY/POWER   PRODUCTIVITY/ENERGY

-10 - 0 - +10 _____   -10 - 0 - +10 _____   -10 - 0 - +10 _____

9AM - ARRIVING AT WORK

INTENT/DESIRE   INTENSITY/POWER   PRODUCTIVITY/ENERGY

-10 - 0 - +10 _____   -10 - 0 - +10 _____   -10 - 0 - +10 _____

1PM - AFTER LUNCH

INTENT/DESIRE   INTENSITY/POWER   PRODUCTIVITY/ENERGY

-10 - 0 - +10 _____   -10 - 0 - +10 _____   -10 - 0 - +10 _____

5PM - WORK DAY END

INTENT/DESIRE   INTENSITY/POWER   PRODUCTIVITY/ENERGY

-10 - 0 - +10 _____   -10 - 0 - +10 _____   -10 - 0 - +10 _____

9PM - BEFORE BED

INTENT/DESIRE   INTENSITY/POWER   PRODUCTIVITY/ENERGY

-10 - 0 - +10 _____   -10 - 0 - +10 _____   -10 - 0 - +10 _____

Chronicles of Change

HIGHS

LOWS

PERSONAL REVELATIONS

DAY # 7

Daily Tracksheet
Success Journal

DAILY TRACKSHEET

6AM - AWAKENING

INTENT/DESIRE   INTENSITY/POWER   PRODUCTIVITY/ENERGY

-10 - 0 - +10 ____   -10 - 0 - +10 ____   -10 - 0 - +10 ____

9AM - ARRIVING AT WORK

INTENT/DESIRE   INTENSITY/POWER   PRODUCTIVITY/ENERGY

-10 - 0 - +10 ____   -10 - 0 - +10 ____   -10 - 0 - +10 ____

1PM - AFTER LUNCH

INTENT/DESIRE   INTENSITY/POWER   PRODUCTIVITY/ENERGY

-10 - 0 - +10 ____   -10 - 0 - +10 ____   -10 - 0 - +10 ____

5PM - WORK DAY END

INTENT/DESIRE   INTENSITY/POWER   PRODUCTIVITY/ENERGY

-10 - 0 - +10 ____   -10 - 0 - +10 ____   -10 - 0 - +10 ____

9PM - BEFORE BED

INTENT/DESIRE   INTENSITY/POWER   PRODUCTIVITY/ENERGY

-10 - 0 - +10 ____   -10 - 0 - +10 ____   -10 - 0 - +10 ____

Chronicles of Change

HIGHS

_____

_____

_____

_____

_____

LOWS

_____

_____

_____

_____

_____

PERSONAL REVELATIONS

DAY # 8

Daily Tracksheet
Success Journal

DAILY TRACKSHEET

6AM - AWAKENING

INTENT/DESIRE   INTENSITY/POWER   PRODUCTIVITY/ENERGY

-10 - 0 - +10 ____   -10 - 0 - +10 ____   -10 - 0 - +10 ____

9AM - ARRIVING AT WORK

INTENT/DESIRE   INTENSITY/POWER   PRODUCTIVITY/ENERGY

-10 - 0 - +10 ____   -10 - 0 - +10 ____   -10 - 0 - +10 ____

1PM - AFTER LUNCH

INTENT/DESIRE   INTENSITY/POWER   PRODUCTIVITY/ENERGY

-10 - 0 - +10 ____   -10 - 0 - +10 ____   -10 - 0 - +10 ____

5PM - WORK DAY END

INTENT/DESIRE   INTENSITY/POWER   PRODUCTIVITY/ENERGY

-10 - 0 - +10 ____   -10 - 0 - +10 ____   -10 - 0 - +10 ____

9PM - BEFORE BED

INTENT/DESIRE   INTENSITY/POWER   PRODUCTIVITY/ENERGY

-10 - 0 - +10 ____   -10 - 0 - +10 ____   -10 - 0 - +10 ____

Chronicles of Change

HIGHS

_____

_____

_____

_____

_____

LOWS

_____

_____

_____

_____

_____

_____

PERSONAL REVELATIONS

DAY # 9

Daily Tracksheet
Success Journal

DAILY TRACKSHEET

6AM - AWAKENING

INTENT/DESIRE   INTENSITY/POWER   PRODUCTIVITY/ENERGY

-10 - 0 - +10 ____   -10 - 0 - +10 ____   -10 - 0 - +10 ____

9AM - ARRIVING AT WORK

INTENT/DESIRE   INTENSITY/POWER   PRODUCTIVITY/ENERGY

-10 - 0 - +10 ____   -10 - 0 - +10 ____   -10 - 0 - +10 ____

1PM - AFTER LUNCH

INTENT/DESIRE   INTENSITY/POWER   PRODUCTIVITY/ENERGY

-10 - 0 - +10 ____   -10 - 0 - +10 ____   -10 - 0 - +10 ____

5PM - WORK DAY END

INTENT/DESIRE   INTENSITY/POWER   PRODUCTIVITY/ENERGY

-10 - 0 - +10 ____   -10 - 0 - +10 ____   -10 - 0 - +10 ____

9PM - BEFORE BED

INTENT/DESIRE   INTENSITY/POWER   PRODUCTIVITY/ENERGY

-10 - 0 - +10 ____   -10 - 0 - +10 ____   -10 - 0 - +10 ____

Chronicles of Change

HIGHS

LOWS

PERSONAL REVELATIONS

DAY # 10

Daily Tracksheet
Success Journal

DAILY TRACKSHEET

6AM - AWAKENING

INTENT/DESIRE   INTENSITY/POWER   PRODUCTIVITY/ENERGY

-10 - 0 - +10 ____   -10 - 0 - +10 ____   -10 - 0 - +10 ____

9AM - ARRIVING AT WORK

INTENT/DESIRE   INTENSITY/POWER   PRODUCTIVITY/ENERGY

-10 - 0 - +10 ____   -10 - 0 - +10 ____   -10 - 0 - +10 ____

1PM - AFTER LUNCH

INTENT/DESIRE   INTENSITY/POWER   PRODUCTIVITY/ENERGY

-10 - 0 - +10 ____   -10 - 0 - +10 ____   -10 - 0 - +10 ____

5PM - WORK DAY END

INTENT/DESIRE   INTENSITY/POWER   PRODUCTIVITY/ENERGY

-10 - 0 - +10 ____   -10 - 0 - +10 ____   -10 - 0 - +10 ____

9PM - BEFORE BED

INTENT/DESIRE   INTENSITY/POWER   PRODUCTIVITY/ENERGY

-10 - 0 - +10 ____   -10 - 0 - +10 ____   -10 - 0 - +10 ____

Chronicles of Change

HIGHS

_____

_____

_____

_____

_____

LOWS

_____

_____

_____

_____

_____

PERSONAL REVELATIONS

DAY #11

Daily Tracksheet
Success Journal

DAILY TRACKSHEET

6AM - AWAKENING

INTENT/DESIRE   INTENSITY/POWER   PRODUCTIVITY/ENERGY

-10 - 0 - +10 _____   -10 - 0 - +10 _____   -10 - 0 - +10 _____

9AM - ARRIVING AT WORK

INTENT/DESIRE   INTENSITY/POWER   PRODUCTIVITY/ENERGY

-10 - 0 - +10 _____   -10 - 0 - +10 _____   -10 - 0 - +10 _____

1PM - AFTER LUNCH

INTENT/DESIRE   INTENSITY/POWER   PRODUCTIVITY/ENERGY

-10 - 0 - +10 _____   -10 - 0 - +10 _____   -10 - 0 - +10 _____

5PM - WORK DAY END

INTENT/DESIRE   INTENSITY/POWER   PRODUCTIVITY/ENERGY

-10 - 0 - +10 _____   -10 - 0 - +10 _____   -10 - 0 - +10 _____

9PM - BEFORE BED

INTENT/DESIRE   INTENSITY/POWER   PRODUCTIVITY/ENERGY

-10 - 0 - +10 _____   -10 - 0 - +10 _____   -10 - 0 - +10 _____

Chronicles of Change

HIGHS

_____

_____

_____

_____

_____

LOWS

_____

_____

_____

_____

_____

PERSONAL REVELATIONS

DAY # 12

Daily Tracksheet
Success Journal

DAILY TRACKSHEET

6AM - AWAKENING

INTENT/DESIRE   INTENSITY/POWER   PRODUCTIVITY/ENERGY

-10 - 0 - +10 ____   -10 - 0 - +10 ____   -10 - 0 - +10 ____

9AM - ARRIVING AT WORK

INTENT/DESIRE   INTENSITY/POWER   PRODUCTIVITY/ENERGY

-10 - 0 - +10 ____   -10 - 0 - +10 ____   -10 - 0 - +10 ____

1PM - AFTER LUNCH

INTENT/DESIRE   INTENSITY/POWER   PRODUCTIVITY/ENERGY

-10 - 0 - +10 ____   -10 - 0 - +10 ____   -10 - 0 - +10 ____

5PM - WORK DAY END

INTENT/DESIRE   INTENSITY/POWER   PRODUCTIVITY/ENERGY

-10 - 0 - +10 ____   -10 - 0 - +10 ____   -10 - 0 - +10 ____

9PM - BEFORE BED

INTENT/DESIRE   INTENSITY/POWER   PRODUCTIVITY/ENERGY

-10 - 0 - +10 ____   -10 - 0 - +10 ____   -10 - 0 - +10 ____

Chronicles of Change

HIGHS

_____

_____

_____

_____

_____

LOWS

_____

_____

_____

_____

_____

PERSONAL REVELATIONS

DAY #13

Daily Tracksheet
Success Journal

DAILY TRACKSHEET

6AM - AWAKENING

INTENT/DESIRE   INTENSITY/POWER   PRODUCTIVITY/ENERGY

-10 - 0 - +10 ____   -10 - 0 - +10 ____   -10 - 0 - +10 ____

9AM - ARRIVING AT WORK

INTENT/DESIRE   INTENSITY/POWER   PRODUCTIVITY/ENERGY

-10 - 0 - +10 ____   -10 - 0 - +10 ____   -10 - 0 - +10 ____

1PM - AFTER LUNCH

INTENT/DESIRE   INTENSITY/POWER   PRODUCTIVITY/ENERGY

-10 - 0 - +10 ____   -10 - 0 - +10 ____   -10 - 0 - +10 ____

5PM - WORK DAY END

INTENT/DESIRE   INTENSITY/POWER   PRODUCTIVITY/ENERGY

-10 - 0 - +10 ____   -10 - 0 - +10 ____   -10 - 0 - +10 ____

9PM - BEFORE BED

INTENT/DESIRE   INTENSITY/POWER   PRODUCTIVITY/ENERGY

-10 - 0 - +10 ____   -10 - 0 - +10 ____   -10 - 0 - +10 ____

Chronicles of Change

HIGHS

LOWS

PERSONAL REVELATIONS

DAY #14

Daily Tracksheet
Success Journal

DAILY TRACKSHEET

6AM - AWAKENING

INTENT/DESIRE   INTENSITY/POWER   PRODUCTIVITY/ENERGY

-10 - 0 - +10 ____   -10 - 0 - +10 ____   -10 - 0 - +10 ____

9AM - ARRIVING AT WORK

INTENT/DESIRE   INTENSITY/POWER   PRODUCTIVITY/ENERGY

-10 - 0 - +10 ____   -10 - 0 - +10 ____   -10 - 0 - +10 ____

1PM - AFTER LUNCH

INTENT/DESIRE   INTENSITY/POWER   PRODUCTIVITY/ENERGY

-10 - 0 - +10 ____   -10 - 0 - +10 ____   -10 - 0 - +10 ____

5PM - WORK DAY END

INTENT/DESIRE   INTENSITY/POWER   PRODUCTIVITY/ENERGY

-10 - 0 - +10 ____   -10 - 0 - +10 ____   -10 - 0 - +10 ____

9PM - BEFORE BED

INTENT/DESIRE   INTENSITY/POWER   PRODUCTIVITY/ENERGY

-10 - 0 - +10 ____   -10 - 0 - +10 ____   -10 - 0 - +10 ____

Chronicles of Change

HIGHS

_____

_____

_____

_____

_____

LOWS

_____

_____

_____

_____

_____

PERSONAL REVELATIONS

DAY # 15

Daily Tracksheet
Success Journal

DAILY TRACKSHEET

6AM - AWAKENING

INTENT/DESIRE   INTENSITY/POWER   PRODUCTIVITY/ENERGY

-10 - 0 - +10 ____   -10 - 0 - +10 ____   -10 - 0 - +10 ____

9AM - ARRIVING AT WORK

INTENT/DESIRE   INTENSITY/POWER   PRODUCTIVITY/ENERGY

-10 - 0 - +10 ____   -10 - 0 - +10 ____   -10 - 0 - +10 ____

1PM - AFTER LUNCH

INTENT/DESIRE   INTENSITY/POWER   PRODUCTIVITY/ENERGY

-10 - 0 - +10 ____   -10 - 0 - +10 ____   -10 - 0 - +10 ____

5PM - WORK DAY END

INTENT/DESIRE   INTENSITY/POWER   PRODUCTIVITY/ENERGY

-10 - 0 - +10 ____   -10 - 0 - +10 ____   -10 - 0 - +10 ____

9PM - BEFORE BED

INTENT/DESIRE   INTENSITY/POWER   PRODUCTIVITY/ENERGY

-10 - 0 - +10 ____   -10 - 0 - +10 ____   -10 - 0 - +10 ____

Chronicles of Change

HIGHS

_____

_____

_____

_____

_____

LOWS

_____

_____

_____

_____

_____

PERSONAL REVELATIONS

DAY # 16

Daily Tracksheet
Success Journal

DAILY TRACKSHEET

6AM - AWAKENING

INTENT/DESIRE   INTENSITY/POWER   PRODUCTIVITY/ENERGY

-10 - 0 - +10 ____   -10 - 0 - +10 ____   -10 - 0 - +10 ____

9AM - ARRIVING AT WORK

INTENT/DESIRE   INTENSITY/POWER   PRODUCTIVITY/ENERGY

-10 - 0 - +10 ____   -10 - 0 - +10 ____   -10 - 0 - +10 ____

1PM - AFTER LUNCH

INTENT/DESIRE   INTENSITY/POWER   PRODUCTIVITY/ENERGY

-10 - 0 - +10 ____   -10 - 0 - +10 ____   -10 - 0 - +10 ____

5PM - WORK DAY END

INTENT/DESIRE   INTENSITY/POWER   PRODUCTIVITY/ENERGY

-10 - 0 - +10 ____   -10 - 0 - +10 ____   -10 - 0 - +10 ____

9PM - BEFORE BED

INTENT/DESIRE   INTENSITY/POWER   PRODUCTIVITY/ENERGY

-10 - 0 - +10 ____   -10 - 0 - +10 ____   -10 - 0 - +10 ____

Chronicles of Change

HIGHS

_____

_____

_____

_____

_____

LOWS

_____

_____

_____

_____

_____

PERSONAL REVELATIONS

DAY # 17

Daily Tracksheet
Success Journal

DAILY TRACKSHEET

6AM - AWAKENING

INTENT/DESIRE   INTENSITY/POWER   PRODUCTIVITY/ENERGY

-10 - 0 - +10 ____   -10 - 0 - +10 ____   -10 - 0 - +10 ____

9AM - ARRIVING AT WORK

INTENT/DESIRE   INTENSITY/POWER   PRODUCTIVITY/ENERGY

-10 - 0 - +10 ____   -10 - 0 - +10 ____   -10 - 0 - +10 ____

1PM - AFTER LUNCH

INTENT/DESIRE   INTENSITY/POWER   PRODUCTIVITY/ENERGY

-10 - 0 - +10 ____   -10 - 0 - +10 ____   -10 - 0 - +10 ____

5PM - WORK DAY END

INTENT/DESIRE   INTENSITY/POWER   PRODUCTIVITY/ENERGY

-10 - 0 - +10 ____   -10 - 0 - +10 ____   -10 - 0 - +10 ____

9PM - BEFORE BED

INTENT/DESIRE   INTENSITY/POWER   PRODUCTIVITY/ENERGY

-10 - 0 - +10 ____   -10 - 0 - +10 ____   -10 - 0 - +10 ____

Chronicles of Change

HIGHS

LOWS

PERSONAL REVELATIONS

DAY # 18

Daily Tracksheet
Success Journal

DAILY TRACKSHEET

6AM - AWAKENING

INTENT/DESIRE   INTENSITY/POWER   PRODUCTIVITY/ENERGY

-10 - 0 - +10 _____   -10 - 0 - +10 _____   -10 - 0 - +10 _____

9AM - ARRIVING AT WORK

INTENT/DESIRE   INTENSITY/POWER   PRODUCTIVITY/ENERGY

-10 - 0 - +10 _____   -10 - 0 - +10 _____   -10 - 0 - +10 _____

1PM - AFTER LUNCH

INTENT/DESIRE   INTENSITY/POWER   PRODUCTIVITY/ENERGY

-10 - 0 - +10 _____   -10 - 0 - +10 _____   -10 - 0 - +10 _____

5PM - WORK DAY END

INTENT/DESIRE   INTENSITY/POWER   PRODUCTIVITY/ENERGY

-10 - 0 - +10 _____   -10 - 0 - +10 _____   -10 - 0 - +10 _____

9PM - BEFORE BED

INTENT/DESIRE   INTENSITY/POWER   PRODUCTIVITY/ENERGY

-10 - 0 - +10 _____   -10 - 0 - +10 _____   -10 - 0 - +10 _____

Chronicles of Change

HIGHS

LOWS

PERSONAL REVELATIONS

DAY # 19

Daily Tracksheet
Success Journal

DAILY TRACKSHEET

6AM - AWAKENING

INTENT/DESIRE　　INTENSITY/POWER　　PRODUCTIVITY/ENERGY

-10 - 0 - +10 _____　　-10 - 0 - +10 _____　　-10 - 0 - +10 _____

9AM - ARRIVING AT WORK

INTENT/DESIRE　　INTENSITY/POWER　　PRODUCTIVITY/ENERGY

-10 - 0 - +10 _____　　-10 - 0 - +10 _____　　-10 - 0 - +10 _____

1PM - AFTER LUNCH

INTENT/DESIRE　　INTENSITY/POWER　　PRODUCTIVITY/ENERGY

-10 - 0 - +10 _____　　-10 - 0 - +10 _____　　-10 - 0 - +10 _____

5PM - WORK DAY END

INTENT/DESIRE　　INTENSITY/POWER　　PRODUCTIVITY/ENERGY

-10 - 0 - +10 _____　　-10 - 0 - +10 _____　　-10 - 0 - +10 _____

9PM - BEFORE BED

INTENT/DESIRE　　INTENSITY/POWER　　PRODUCTIVITY/ENERGY

-10 - 0 - +10 _____　　-10 - 0 - +10 _____　　-10 - 0 - +10 _____

Chronicles of Change

HIGHS

LOWS

PERSONAL REVELATIONS

DAY # 20

Daily Tracksheet
Success Journal

DAILY TRACKSHEET

6AM - AWAKENING

INTENT/DESIRE   INTENSITY/POWER   PRODUCTIVITY/ENERGY

-10 - 0 - +10 ____   -10 - 0 - +10 ____   -10 - 0 - +10 ____

9AM - ARRIVING AT WORK

INTENT/DESIRE   INTENSITY/POWER   PRODUCTIVITY/ENERGY

-10 - 0 - +10 ____   -10 - 0 - +10 ____   -10 - 0 - +10 ____

1PM - AFTER LUNCH

INTENT/DESIRE   INTENSITY/POWER   PRODUCTIVITY/ENERGY

-10 - 0 - +10 ____   -10 - 0 - +10 ____   -10 - 0 - +10 ____

5PM - WORK DAY END

INTENT/DESIRE   INTENSITY/POWER   PRODUCTIVITY/ENERGY

-10 - 0 - +10 ____   -10 - 0 - +10 ____   -10 - 0 - +10 ____

9PM - BEFORE BED

INTENT/DESIRE   INTENSITY/POWER   PRODUCTIVITY/ENERGY

-10 - 0 - +10 ____   -10 - 0 - +10 ____   -10 - 0 - +10 ____

Chronicles of Change

HIGHS

_____
_____
_____
_____
_____

LOWS

_____
_____
_____
_____
_____

PERSONAL REVELATIONS

DAY # 21

Daily Tracksheet
Success Journal

DAILY TRACKSHEET

6AM - AWAKENING

INTENT/DESIRE   INTENSITY/POWER   PRODUCTIVITY/ENERGY

-10 - 0 - +10 ____   -10 - 0 - +10 ____   -10 - 0 - +10 ____

9AM - ARRIVING AT WORK

INTENT/DESIRE   INTENSITY/POWER   PRODUCTIVITY/ENERGY

-10 - 0 - +10 ____   -10 - 0 - +10 ____   -10 - 0 - +10 ____

1PM - AFTER LUNCH

INTENT/DESIRE   INTENSITY/POWER   PRODUCTIVITY/ENERGY

-10 - 0 - +10 ____   -10 - 0 - +10 ____   -10 - 0 - +10 ____

5PM - WORK DAY END

INTENT/DESIRE   INTENSITY/POWER   PRODUCTIVITY/ENERGY

-10 - 0 - +10 ____   -10 - 0 - +10 ____   -10 - 0 - +10 ____

9PM - BEFORE BED

INTENT/DESIRE   INTENSITY/POWER   PRODUCTIVITY/ENERGY

-10 - 0 - +10 ____   -10 - 0 - +10 ____   -10 - 0 - +10 ____

Chronicles of Change

HIGHS

_____

_____

_____

_____

_____

LOWS

_____

_____

_____

_____

_____

PERSONAL REVELATIONS

DAY # 22

Daily Tracksheet
Success Journal

DAILY TRACKSHEET

6AM - AWAKENING

INTENT/DESIRE   INTENSITY/POWER   PRODUCTIVITY/ENERGY

-10 - 0 - +10 ____   -10 - 0 - +10 ____   -10 - 0 - +10 ____

9AM - ARRIVING AT WORK

INTENT/DESIRE   INTENSITY/POWER   PRODUCTIVITY/ENERGY

-10 - 0 - +10 ____   -10 - 0 - +10 ____   -10 - 0 - +10 ____

1PM - AFTER LUNCH

INTENT/DESIRE   INTENSITY/POWER   PRODUCTIVITY/ENERGY

-10 - 0 - +10 ____   -10 - 0 - +10 ____   -10 - 0 - +10 ____

5PM - WORK DAY END

INTENT/DESIRE   INTENSITY/POWER   PRODUCTIVITY/ENERGY

-10 - 0 - +10 ____   -10 - 0 - +10 ____   -10 - 0 - +10 ____

9PM - BEFORE BED

INTENT/DESIRE   INTENSITY/POWER   PRODUCTIVITY/ENERGY

-10 - 0 - +10 ____   -10 - 0 - +10 ____   -10 - 0 - +10 ____

Chronicles of Change

HIGHS

LOWS

PERSONAL REVELATIONS

DAY # 23

Daily Tracksheet
Success Journal

DAILY TRACKSHEET

6AM - AWAKENING

INTENT/DESIRE   INTENSITY/POWER   PRODUCTIVITY/ENERGY

-10 - 0 - +10 ____   -10 - 0 - +10 ____   -10 - 0 - +10 ____

9AM - ARRIVING AT WORK

INTENT/DESIRE   INTENSITY/POWER   PRODUCTIVITY/ENERGY

-10 - 0 - +10 ____   -10 - 0 - +10 ____   -10 - 0 - +10 ____

1PM - AFTER LUNCH

INTENT/DESIRE   INTENSITY/POWER   PRODUCTIVITY/ENERGY

-10 - 0 - +10 ____   -10 - 0 - +10 ____   -10 - 0 - +10 ____

5PM - WORK DAY END

INTENT/DESIRE   INTENSITY/POWER   PRODUCTIVITY/ENERGY

-10 - 0 - +10 ____   -10 - 0 - +10 ____   -10 - 0 - +10 ____

9PM - BEFORE BED

INTENT/DESIRE   INTENSITY/POWER   PRODUCTIVITY/ENERGY

-10 - 0 - +10 ____   -10 - 0 - +10 ____   -10 - 0 - +10 ____

Chronicles of Change

HIGHS

_____

_____

_____

_____

_____

LOWS

_____

_____

_____

_____

_____

PERSONAL REVELATIONS

DAY # 24

Daily Tracksheet
Success Journal

DAILY TRACKSHEET

6AM - AWAKENING

INTENT/DESIRE   INTENSITY/POWER   PRODUCTIVITY/ENERGY

-10 - 0 - +10 _____   -10 - 0 - +10 _____   -10 - 0 - +10 _____

9AM - ARRIVING AT WORK

INTENT/DESIRE   INTENSITY/POWER   PRODUCTIVITY/ENERGY

-10 - 0 - +10 _____   -10 - 0 - +10 _____   -10 - 0 - +10 _____

1PM - AFTER LUNCH

INTENT/DESIRE   INTENSITY/POWER   PRODUCTIVITY/ENERGY

-10 - 0 - +10 _____   -10 - 0 - +10 _____   -10 - 0 - +10 _____

5PM - WORK DAY END

INTENT/DESIRE   INTENSITY/POWER   PRODUCTIVITY/ENERGY

-10 - 0 - +10 _____   -10 - 0 - +10 _____   -10 - 0 - +10 _____

9PM - BEFORE BED

INTENT/DESIRE   INTENSITY/POWER   PRODUCTIVITY/ENERGY

-10 - 0 - +10 _____   -10 - 0 - +10 _____   -10 - 0 - +10 _____

Chronicles of Change

HIGHS

_____

_____

_____

_____

_____

LOWS

_____

_____

_____

_____

_____

PERSONAL REVELATIONS

DAY # 25

Daily Tracksheet
Success Journal

DAILY TRACKSHEET

6AM - AWAKENING

INTENT/DESIRE   INTENSITY/POWER   PRODUCTIVITY/ENERGY

-10 - 0 - +10 ____   -10 - 0 - +10 ____   -10 - 0 - +10 ____

9AM - ARRIVING AT WORK

INTENT/DESIRE   INTENSITY/POWER   PRODUCTIVITY/ENERGY

-10 - 0 - +10 ____   -10 - 0 - +10 ____   -10 - 0 - +10 ____

1PM - AFTER LUNCH

INTENT/DESIRE   INTENSITY/POWER   PRODUCTIVITY/ENERGY

-10 - 0 - +10 ____   -10 - 0 - +10 ____   -10 - 0 - +10 ____

5PM - WORK DAY END

INTENT/DESIRE   INTENSITY/POWER   PRODUCTIVITY/ENERGY

-10 - 0 - +10 ____   -10 - 0 - +10 ____   -10 - 0 - +10 ____

9PM - BEFORE BED

INTENT/DESIRE   INTENSITY/POWER   PRODUCTIVITY/ENERGY

-10 - 0 - +10 ____   -10 - 0 - +10 ____   -10 - 0 - +10 ____

Chronicles of Change

HIGHS

_____

_____

_____

_____

_____

LOWS

_____

_____

_____

_____

_____

PERSONAL REVELATIONS

DAY # 26

Daily Tracksheet
Success Journal

DAILY TRACKSHEET

6AM - AWAKENING

INTENT/DESIRE   INTENSITY/POWER   PRODUCTIVITY/ENERGY

-10 - 0 - +10 ____   -10 - 0 - +10 ____   -10 - 0 - +10 ____

9AM - ARRIVING AT WORK

INTENT/DESIRE   INTENSITY/POWER   PRODUCTIVITY/ENERGY

-10 - 0 - +10 ____   -10 - 0 - +10 ____   -10 - 0 - +10 ____

1PM - AFTER LUNCH

INTENT/DESIRE   INTENSITY/POWER   PRODUCTIVITY/ENERGY

-10 - 0 - +10 ____   -10 - 0 - +10 ____   -10 - 0 - +10 ____

5PM - WORK DAY END

INTENT/DESIRE   INTENSITY/POWER   PRODUCTIVITY/ENERGY

-10 - 0 - +10 ____   -10 - 0 - +10 ____   -10 - 0 - +10 ____

9PM - BEFORE BED

INTENT/DESIRE   INTENSITY/POWER   PRODUCTIVITY/ENERGY

-10 - 0 - +10 ____   -10 - 0 - +10 ____   -10 - 0 - +10 ____

Chronicles of Change

HIGHS

_____

_____

_____

_____

_____

LOWS

_____

_____

_____

_____

_____

PERSONAL REVELATIONS

DAY # 27

Daily Tracksheet
Success Journal

DAILY TRACKSHEET

6AM - AWAKENING

INTENT/DESIRE   INTENSITY/POWER   PRODUCTIVITY/ENERGY

-10 - 0 - +10 ____   -10 - 0 - +10 ____   -10 - 0 - +10 ____

9AM - ARRIVING AT WORK

INTENT/DESIRE   INTENSITY/POWER   PRODUCTIVITY/ENERGY

-10 - 0 - +10 ____   -10 - 0 - +10 ____   -10 - 0 - +10 ____

1PM - AFTER LUNCH

INTENT/DESIRE   INTENSITY/POWER   PRODUCTIVITY/ENERGY

-10 - 0 - +10 ____   -10 - 0 - +10 ____   -10 - 0 - +10 ____

5PM - WORK DAY END

INTENT/DESIRE   INTENSITY/POWER   PRODUCTIVITY/ENERGY

-10 - 0 - +10 ____   -10 - 0 - +10 ____   -10 - 0 - +10 ____

9PM - BEFORE BED

INTENT/DESIRE   INTENSITY/POWER   PRODUCTIVITY/ENERGY

-10 - 0 - +10 ____   -10 - 0 - +10 ____   -10 - 0 - +10 ____

Chronicles of Change

HIGHS

LOWS

PERSONAL REVELATIONS

DAY # 28

Daily Tracksheet
Success Journal

DAILY TRACKSHEET

6AM - AWAKENING

INTENT/DESIRE   INTENSITY/POWER   PRODUCTIVITY/ENERGY

-10 - 0 - +10 _____   -10 - 0 - +10 _____   -10 - 0 - +10 _____

9AM - ARRIVING AT WORK

INTENT/DESIRE   INTENSITY/POWER   PRODUCTIVITY/ENERGY

-10 - 0 - +10 _____   -10 - 0 - +10 _____   -10 - 0 - +10 _____

1PM - AFTER LUNCH

INTENT/DESIRE   INTENSITY/POWER   PRODUCTIVITY/ENERGY

-10 - 0 - +10 _____   -10 - 0 - +10 _____   -10 - 0 - +10 _____

5PM - WORK DAY END

INTENT/DESIRE   INTENSITY/POWER   PRODUCTIVITY/ENERGY

-10 - 0 - +10 _____   -10 - 0 - +10 _____   -10 - 0 - +10 _____

9PM - BEFORE BED

INTENT/DESIRE   INTENSITY/POWER   PRODUCTIVITY/ENERGY

-10 - 0 - +10 _____   -10 - 0 - +10 _____   -10 - 0 - +10 _____

Chronicles of Change

HIGHS

_____

_____

_____

_____

_____

LOWS

_____

_____

_____

_____

_____

PERSONAL REVELATIONS

DAY # 29

Daily Tracksheet
Success Journal

DAILY TRACKSHEET

6AM - AWAKENING

INTENT/DESIRE   INTENSITY/POWER   PRODUCTIVITY/ENERGY

-10 - 0 - +10 ____   -10 - 0 - +10 ____   -10 - 0 - +10 ____

9AM - ARRIVING AT WORK

INTENT/DESIRE   INTENSITY/POWER   PRODUCTIVITY/ENERGY

-10 - 0 - +10 ____   -10 - 0 - +10 ____   -10 - 0 - +10 ____

1PM - AFTER LUNCH

INTENT/DESIRE   INTENSITY/POWER   PRODUCTIVITY/ENERGY

-10 - 0 - +10 ____   -10 - 0 - +10 ____   -10 - 0 - +10 ____

5PM - WORK DAY END

INTENT/DESIRE   INTENSITY/POWER   PRODUCTIVITY/ENERGY

-10 - 0 - +10 ____   -10 - 0 - +10 ____   -10 - 0 - +10 ____

9PM - BEFORE BED

INTENT/DESIRE   INTENSITY/POWER   PRODUCTIVITY/ENERGY

-10 - 0 - +10 ____   -10 - 0 - +10 ____   -10 - 0 - +10 ____

Chronicles of Change

HIGHS

_____
_____
_____
_____

LOWS

_____
_____
_____
_____

PERSONAL REVELATIONS

DAY # 30

Daily Tracksheet
Success Journal

DAILY TRACKSHEET

6AM - AWAKENING

INTENT/DESIRE   INTENSITY/POWER   PRODUCTIVITY/ENERGY

-10 - 0 - +10 ____   -10 - 0 - +10 ____   -10 - 0 - +10 ____

9AM - ARRIVING AT WORK

INTENT/DESIRE   INTENSITY/POWER   PRODUCTIVITY/ENERGY

-10 - 0 - +10 ____   -10 - 0 - +10 ____   -10 - 0 - +10 ____

1PM - AFTER LUNCH

INTENT/DESIRE   INTENSITY/POWER   PRODUCTIVITY/ENERGY

-10 - 0 - +10 ____   -10 - 0 - +10 ____   -10 - 0 - +10 ____

5PM - WORK DAY END

INTENT/DESIRE   INTENSITY/POWER   PRODUCTIVITY/ENERGY

-10 - 0 - +10 ____   -10 - 0 - +10 ____   -10 - 0 - +10 ____

9PM - BEFORE BED

INTENT/DESIRE   INTENSITY/POWER   PRODUCTIVITY/ENERGY

-10 - 0 - +10 ____   -10 - 0 - +10 ____   -10 - 0 - +10 ____

Chronicles of Change

HIGHS

_____
_____
_____
_____
_____

LOWS

_____
_____
_____
_____
_____

PERSONAL REVELATIONS

About the Author

NATAN VERKHOVSKY, M.Ht

Born in the former USSR and immigrating to Calgary, Alberta Canada, with his family as a small child, Natan began a 30 (plus) year journey into Martial Arts. At 15 he took up the sport of Power Tumbling and rose to be ranked #1 in his division in Alberta.

Developing his mental training skills, he pursued an education in Medical Hypnotherapy, under the tutelage of Dr. Michael Preston, Director of the Institute of Medical Hypnotherapy, in Phoenix Arizona.

After becoming certified in his early 20's, Natan began working with his Team 2000 Olympic Men's Gymnastic team mates, and other artists and elite athletes from Cirque Du Soleil, as a Mental Training Specialist. It was around this time that he developed the program Personal Momentum.

Since then, he has developed and adapted 23 Mental, Physical & Emotional drills and exercises to help Peak Performers in all disciplines and walks of life. Working with some of the most successful and challenging individuals and groups, giving concrete and actionable peak performance coaching, is what separates Natan Verkhovsky from others. He offers two things needed for your change to be truly transformational: Accountability and Transformational Tools.

He is the director of The Essential Academy, a learning platform for people who are passionate about continued growth and learning. No matter what your age or experience, The Essential Academy offers elite training courses to take your life to the next level.

Find out more at :   https://www.essentialacademy.org

www.ingramcontent.com/pod-product-compliance
Lightning Source LLC
Chambersburg PA
CBHW050310010526
44107CB00055B/2176